THE POWER

OF

KNOWING

GOD

TONY EVANS

HARVEST HOUSE PUBLISHERS
EUGENE, OREGON

Interior design by Angie Renich / Wildwood Digital Publishing

Cover design by Bryce Williamson

Cover photo (c) Andrea Fontanili / EyeEm / Gettyimages

The Power of Knowing God
Copyright © 2020 by Tony Evans
Published by Harvest House Publishers
Eugene, Oregon 97408
www.harvesthousepublishers.com

ISBN 978-0-7369-6954-3 (pbk.)
ISBN 978-0-7369-6955-0 (eBook)

Names: Evans, Tony, author.
Title: The Power of Knowing God / Tony Evans.
Description: Eugene, Oregon : Harvest House Publishers, 2020. | Summary:
   "Tony Evans believes knowing God fully should be everyone's life
   pursuit. He has developed a strategy for living victoriously as a child
   of God and he wants to equip you with the right tools for achieving an
   authentic relationship with the Savior"-- Provided by publisher.
Identifiers: LCCN 2019060273 (print) | LCCN 2019060274 (ebook) | ISBN
   9780736969543 (paperback) | ISBN 9780736969550 (ebook)
Subjects: LCSH: God (Christianity)--Worship and love. | God
   (Christianity)--Knowableness.
Classification: LCC BV4817 .E925 2020 (print) | LCC BV4817 (ebook) | DDC
   231/.042--dc23
LC record available at https://lccn.loc.gov/2019060273
LC ebook record available at https://lccn.loc.gov/2019060274

Printed in the United States of America

20 21 22 23 24 25 26 27 28 / BP-AR / 10 9 8 7 6 5 4 3 2 1

Contents

Acknowledgments

I want to thank my friends at Harvest House Publishers for their long-standing partnership in bringing my thoughts, study, and words to print. I particularly want to thank Bob Hawkins for his friendship over the years, as well as his pursuit of excellence in leading his company. I also want to publicly thank Terry Glaspey, Betty Fletcher, and Amber Holcomb for their help in the editorial process. In addition, my appreciation goes out to Heather Hair for her skills and insights in collaboration on this manuscript.

Part 1

THE PURSUIT

1

LIFE'S HIGHEST AIM

A number of years ago, I was invited to do something I had never done before: skeet shooting. The goal of skeet shooting is to take a shotgun and try to hit little clay disks that get flung out of a machine into the air.

I'm from the concrete jungle of Baltimore, and I later moved to another metropolitan area called Dallas. Before being invited to go skeet shooting, I'd never gone hunting or target shooting before. But the concept was intriguing, and in all honesty the sport didn't look that difficult as I watched the man who had invited me knock disk after disk out of the sky.

Being the man that I am, I quickly walked over to the gun, picked it up, and aimed. I didn't need any lessons. That disk was mine, and it was coming down. Placing the gun against my shoulder, I proceeded to consistently miss my target.

Time after time I shot into the air like a starter announcing the beginning of a race. Regardless of how I aimed or where I looked, my efforts were in vain. I was in the right place and I was holding the right tools, but I wasn't making the connection. I failed to achieve my goal.

After enough rounds of wasted shot, my friend approached and asked if he could be of any assistance. I swallowed my pride for a moment and nodded my head. He then explained that when the disks are shot out of the machine, they move at a rapid pace. Because of this speed, the way to hit them is to get out in front of them. He instructed me never to aim at the disk itself, but to always aim a foot or two in front of it. That way, when the pellet reaches its destination, it will be in the same position as the clay disk.

Taking just a bit of advice from someone who knew what they were talking about enabled me to shoot my first disk clear out of the sky. And then my next one, and my next, and my next.

WHEN SOMETHING IS MISSING

Friend, if you go to church, read your Bible, and participate in Bible study groups, you have the right tools for living the victorious Christian life. But even when you have the right tools or position yourself in the right place, there still seems to be something missing.

Far too many believers today are living off target. It's not for a lack of effort. Neither is it for a lack of concentration. And it's certainly not because they are insincere. It's something deeper than all of that.

For example, when I attempted to hit the disks in the sky that brisk morning, I tried very hard. I focused very hard. But I still came up empty because I just didn't know the strategy for success. Once I discovered that strategy, I shot disk after disk out of the clear blue sky.

Similarly, there exists a strategy in the Christian life that few people ever realize. Despite their best attempts at living the abundant life Christ died to secure for them, they fall short. And even though the strategy requires very little external adjustment on their part, when that adjustment is made, it makes all the difference in the world.

What is this strategy to living out the fullness of your victory as a child of the King? It involves how well you know God.

Knowing God ought to be your life's greatest pursuit.

HOW WELL DO YOU KNOW GOD?

There are a variety of ways that people get to know God. Some people don't know Him at all because they are unconverted and unsaved. But then there are those who know Him casually. He is an acquaintance to them. Yes, they believe in Him and check in with Him from time to time. They'll "like" a Scripture here or there or "comment" on Him at church or in social circles, but they really don't know Him that well at all.

Other people know God informationally. They talk about Him fairly regularly and expound on their knowledge of Him. They may read a number of books on Him or hear a lot of sermons about Him. They could give you an in-depth description of His stories, history, and qualities. They are relatively sound on who God is. They may even have a working knowledge of Bible doctrine.

There are others who know Him religiously and, in a way, He has become very programmatic to them because they connect to Him through activities, duties, or service.

Then there are those who know God spiritually. They can tell you how it feels when the Holy Spirit moves around or in them. They can emotively describe the feelings believing and hoping in God gives them.

As you can see, there are a number of different approaches and ways of understanding or knowing God. But none of these ways are what I am talking about in this book. Now, the path we are going to look at together will include a number of attributes from each of these categories, sure, but it will go deeper than that. While knowing God does involve your intellect, emotions, and actions, it also involves so much more. Because intellect, emotions, and actions on their own do not comprise the true meaning of knowing.

Consider a husband and wife who have been married for four or five decades. Of course, by then they intellectually know their spouse, they emotionally grasp how he or she makes them feel, and they have made adjustments in their actions in an effort to align with their spouse's desires. However, even with those three aspects of knowing, they may not truly know each other at all.

You've seen them. These couples can predict each other's next word, and they'll dutifully accompany each other to whatever appointment or experience is on the agenda, but something seems to be missing. Despite years together and shared memories, they are still not connected in the way that matters most.

Knowing someone—even knowing God—involves much more than simple knowledge. It involves a connection so authentic and real that it gives birth to a synchronicity and cadence established as a natural outgrowth of the relationship itself. Knowing someone often can't be defined in words or activities. It's that subtle savoring that occurs within two souls uniquely bonded in love.

Our foundational passage for understanding why we are to pursue knowing God intimately is Jeremiah 9:23-24, where we read,

> Thus says the LORD, "Let not a wise man boast of his wisdom, and let not the mighty man boast of his might, let not a rich man boast of his riches; but let him who boasts boast of this, that he understands and knows Me."

When a man sees a lady who captures his imagination, and he walks over to ask her, "What's your name?" he is after much more than information. While information is necessary, that's not his goal. His goal is a relationship. As this man and woman begin to date and start talking on the phone, facts about each other transform into feelings. As these feelings deepen, he becomes moved to ask for her hand in marriage. When she says yes and the wedding occurs, they then spend their first night together on their honeymoon. When the feelings have culminated in a mutual love, they then initiate the full knowing of each other in their first time of intimacy together.

See, that's what the Bible says when we read in Genesis 4:1, "Now Adam knew Eve his wife, and she conceived and bore Cain" (ESV). When the Bible talks about people knowing each other in this biblical sense, it is referring to physical intimacy at its greatest level. This ushers in the ability to both know and be known—which involves much more than mere physical contact and is only attainable in an atmosphere of total and deserved trust.

The Hebrew term used in Genesis 4:1 is the word *yada*. It is the same word used a few verses earlier when describing how Adam's and Eve's eyes had been opened and they "knew" they were naked (Genesis 3:7). It is also the same word used in Genesis 3:22, where we read, "The LORD God said, 'Behold, the man has become like one of Us, knowing good and evil.'"

The word *yada* is not a word referring to body parts or physical activity. In all definitions of the word *yada*, which occurs more than 1,000 times in the Old Testament, it means:

- to know or learn to know
- to be made known or revealed
- to make oneself known to another
- to cause someone to know
- to know based on experience[1]

When *yada* is used in connection with relational interaction, it indicates plumbing the depths of someone else's reality. In fact, it has the capacity to be so intimate a term when applied to relational involvement that God uses it to refer to His own relationship with us.

> The secret of the LORD is for those who fear Him, and He will make them know [*yada*] His covenant (Psalm 25:14).

> "You are My witnesses," declares the LORD, "and My servant whom I have chosen, so that you may know [*yada*] and believe Me" (Isaiah 43:10).

> I will give you the treasures of darkness and hidden wealth of secret places, so that you may know [*yada*] that it is I, the LORD, the God of Israel, who calls you by your name (Isaiah 45:3).

In each of these descriptions, God speaks of His relationship with humankind in a close and intimate manner. We read about "treasures of darkness," being "chosen," and God's self-obligatory relationship He establishes called His "covenant." On top of that, twice we read the specific word *secret*—once in reference to God's secrets ("the secret of the LORD") and also in relation to what God will give ("hidden wealth of secret places").

One thing about secrets is that you have to be pretty close in order to share them. Of course, you have to be close emotionally by way of trust, but oftentimes secret sharing includes being close in proximity as well.

When you were younger and wanted to tell someone a secret, what would you normally do? If you were like me, you would move next to the other person, close enough so that you could lean over and, with your hand cupped around your mouth, whisper in his or her ear.

That is the typical way of sharing a secret.

And that is what God says He will do with those who know (*yada*) Him. He will be so close that you can hear Him whispering in your ear, telling you the secrets that are reserved for those who have a special relationship of intimacy with Him.

Yet, what is essential to realize is that when God chose to *yada* us, He chose to do so with a people who are perishing (John 3:16), have gone astray (Luke 19:10), and are condemned (John 3:18). God gave His perfection to those who knew only imperfection (Romans 3:23). He revealed the purity of Himself to those who are "desperately wicked" (Jeremiah 17:9 KJV). And He was able to do all of this while maintaining His holiness, because Jesus hung on a cross as a sacrifice for the sins of us all. Jesus not only died physically, but He died to Himself, as we read, "He humbled Himself by becoming obedient to the point of death, even death on a cross" (Philippians 2:8).

Likewise, the very foundation of true relationship with God Himself is rooted in a sacrificial dying to yourself, laying your will, pride, and needs on the altar while considering God's heart as more important than your own. Knowing God involves so much more than just looking to Him as a cosmic Santa Claus or an emotional ride. Knowing God involves sacrifice on your part as well. Knowing Him means sharing your secrets, your heart's DNA, your fears, your hopes, your failures, and even your "treasures of darkness and hidden wealth of secret places" (Isaiah 45:3). It involves revealing yourself in a way unlike you do with any other. And within that revelation, you will find the most authentic form of love possible.

In fact, the secret nature of what you share with God becomes its own treasure.

So we're not talking about meeting God, gaining information about God, or even "dating" God. We're talking about getting to know the depths of His being and being absorbed in Him. God is your friend, yes, but He's interested in much, much more than that. He is interested in intimacy at the highest level.

RICHES, WISDOM, AND MIGHT

The context surrounding the passage we looked at earlier in Jeremiah 9 is very interesting. It includes the Babylonian captivity of the Israelites as well as a significant amount of chaos in the land. In the midst of this turmoil, God arrives to provide stability and comfort. But He does this by pointing out that they are after the wrong things, which are summarized in three words: *riches*, *wisdom*, and *might*.

To contemporize these three words, we would say *riches* mean a big bank account; *wisdom* means plenty of degrees on the wall; and *might* means power, prominence, and platform. Essentially, these are the three things that nearly every American wants as well—to earn as much as they can, go as high as they can, and climb the ladder of success. But what God says is that if your claim to fame is your master's degree or the fact that you have the most powerful platform in your circle, then you've really got nothing to brag about at all. Because all of that, from God's overarching perspective, means little compared to what matters most.

Returning to the marriage analogy, this truth may make better sense if we compare it to a husband and wife team where one spouse is highly successful, brings home a lot of money, waxes eloquent on a number of topics, and can essentially work any room. But if the marriage lacks the all-encompassing element of intimate love, not only will all of that mean little to nothing, it may even crop up as a point of dissension and resentment. A sincere woman doesn't marry a man for his paycheck or business card, and vice versa. Couples marry because they love each other and want that love to be an integral part of their lives.

When God sees us striving after status at the expense of relishing our relationship with Him, He feels like a jilted lover to some extent (James 4:4-5). After all, it is He who enables us to accomplish anything (Deuteronomy 8:18). And while riches, wisdom, and might are not wrong in and of themselves, they become wrong when they are pursued at the expense of intimacy with God. If you know the line items in your bank account better than you know the heart of God, that's wrong. If everybody knows your name, but you don't know the attributes of God's names and how they intricately link with your soul, that's wrong. Riches, wisdom, and might must be kept in their proper place. All boasting about them amounts to naught.

It reminds me of the story of a woodpecker that was pecking at a tree. He kept pecking and pecking and pecking until one day lightning came along, hit the tree, and split it right in two. The woodpecker thought he was Mr. Big Stuff until something bigger and more powerful showed up. In our social-media culture, it's easy to believe our own reviews and start thinking we are something bigger than we actually are. But none of what we accomplish ever originates solely in us. We are all here by the grace of God and empowered by that same grace.

God didn't condemn boasting in the Jeremiah passage. No, He wants you to be confident. He wants you to be vocal. He wants you to go public. What He did condemn was boasting in the wrong things. God wants you to boast that you know Him intimately, fully, completely—like an engaged woman who goes on and on and on about her fiancé's qualities and character. God wants you to understand and know Him that well. We read in Jeremiah 9:24, "Let him who boasts boast of this, that he understands and knows Me, that I am the LORD who exercises lovingkindness, justice and righteousness on earth; for I delight in these things."

THE FULL EFFECT

God wants you to talk about who He is. And not just who He is in the heavens. He wants you to know Him in history, on earth. It's not a long-distance relationship God is after. He wants you to know His ways, His moves, His heart, and what He does on earth so well that you can't help but tell it to others. God desires to reveal Himself to you in such a way that makes you smile with delight. That's called "illumination." Illumination is when God unveils Himself and allows you to see Him for who He truly is.

It's like when you have a dimmer attached to a light in a room. Turning on the light allows for a portion of that light to illuminate the room, but as you turn the dial even more, additional light brightens the room. The greater the illumination, the more easily you can see everything there is to be seen.

If you are going to really get to know God, then He must have the freedom to provide full illumination of Himself so that you can see who He truly is, not who you have boxed Him into being. So many people have preconceived notions of who God is. They place Him in their neat little box tied with neat little strings and say, "He's like that" and "He's like this." But one thing I know beyond any doubt after living more than seven decades on this earth is that God is not always who we think He is. His ways are beyond ours (Isaiah 55:9). His character allows for so much more than we think. His depth goes further than we can bear. He has surprised me, shocked me, and even charmed me at times. He has a sense of humor. His emotions are bottomless. And His jealousy is strong. He's a romantic, a dramatist, and an artist, while simultaneously being the greatest mathematician, scientist, and logician.

Problems arise when we fail to allow God to be God, when we put Him in our tidy tin can and say, "Come out when I need You." I admit, that would be a convenient god. In fact, most people don't want a God who truly unveils Himself because it can be frightening, startling, and unpredictable. But when you choose to label God or diagnose Him, you no longer have the true, relational God—you have an idol which you yourself have created.

Only God gets to define Himself. And only God gets to reveal who He is and how He operates in history. He is who He is, not who you say He is.

Do you know what keeps people from knowing God? They do not simply allow Him to be God because they impose their own understanding, expectations, and desires onto Him.

God has a résumé. Sixty-six books in total. It's thick! When we read His résumé, the Bible, we should respond with, "Wow, He's got a lot of experience." Not only that, He also has references—people all over the world who talk about Him and what He has done in and through them.

But it's normal after someone has received a résumé and checked the references to say that they want an interview as well. Because while the written document is good and what other people are saying is nice, they want to see this person for themselves.

See, a lot of Christians are satisfied with simply reading God's résumé. So they come to church every Sunday and say, "Read me some more of your résumé, God! It's really impressive." But the problem is that some Christians stop at the résumé or the references, the testimonies of those who have known God for themselves. But God is waiting on the interview. He wants the face-to-face meeting because He wants you to know Him as He knows and loves you. He wants you to experience Him for yourself.

Have you ever watched a movie at the theater and then gone back a second time and experienced it in 3-D? Once you see it in 3-D, you realize that you didn't really see it much at all the first time. This is because you pick up on nuances in 3-D that have been designed to be revealed only in that unique format. What's more, if you decide to go and watch the movie in IMAX 3-D, it comes right off the screen, and you feel like you have to turn your head just to catch it all. This is because you are now seeing things from a different dimension.

When God calls us to know and experience Him, He's not

satisfied with a regular viewing or connection. He doesn't want us to have merely an HD view of who He is. No, He wants us to feel the full effect of IMAX 3-D, where everywhere we turn our gaze, He's there—all around us in every way.

As we start this quest together in our study on the power of knowing God, your challenge is to give Him the opportunity to give you *His* terms on how to get to know Him best. That is how you will come to know Him as He really is, and not simply as you have been taught or have come to expect Him to be. Then, as you respond to what He reveals to you, the door will open for Him to show you so much more of Himself. Remember, God wants more than a fan club. He wants an intimate relationship with you.

2

HOW BAD
DO YOU
WANT IT?

When a sports team is ready to head into competition, they're regularly asked, "How bad do you want it?"

It's a question about desire. It's a question about drive. It's not a question about skill, preparation, or strategy. Rather, it's a question about passion and need—even craving.

The answer to this question will often make or break a player or team. Drive and desire count for much more than we often realize.

This question doesn't only apply to sports. It can be asked of an employee about their job. It can be asked of a relationship or a marriage. It can be asked of many things. Because we all know that when somebody wants something very badly, they will often stop at nothing to accomplish it. Whether it's a goal, challenge, dream, vision, or relationship—desire drives results.

When it comes to knowing God, this is a question that will define everything.

God truly wants to know how bad you want Him. Are you satisfied with a cavalier god? Are you happy with a casual relationship? Or do you long for something more—something with fire, passion, electricity, and energy?

Far too many believers are satisfied with simply being church goers on their way to heaven. As a result, they can never talk about their experience with God. They don't truly know Him as He desires to be known. This is because knowing God comes through effort, pursuit, and desire, not merely flipping open your Bible and looking for a verse a day to keep the devil away. Knowing God involves an intentional quest for intimacy.

One of the reasons you need to be intentional in your pursuit of God is that there is a lot of opposition toward you growing close to Him. A number of things get in the way of experiencing God on earth, such as challenges in life, time constraints, and issues that limit your capacity for intimacy. Distractions could also include entertainment like television, social media, internet browsing, and sports. While none of these things are bad in and of themselves, when you compile them all together and look back over how much of your attention and effort is spent on them, you might be surprised at what you find. It is possible to be so full from enjoying junk food that you lose your appetite for what truly satisfies.

There is an app that was created for those who struggle with too much social media screen time. This app monitors how much time a person spends on each of the different social media channels. The user can set a predetermined limit on how much time they want to spend on social media, and when that limit is reached, the app blocks their access for the rest of the day. This app helps those who struggle with addictive behaviors or who simply need to pull back.

But I wonder what an app would look like that tracks how much time we spend pursuing all our interests in life. Whether it's television, online shopping, reading, or pursuing God, a bar would tally our time and we could check it at the end of the day. I wonder if we would be surprised to see how we actually do spend our time—and how very little God often gets from us.

One of the questions a doctor will ask you if you show up in her office not feeling well or facing some health issues in your life is about the state of your appetite. This is because doctors know that if there is an ongoing loss of hunger, something deeper is wrong. Far too many of us have lost our appetites when it comes to knowing God. We've become satisfied with a snack here or a sip there. As a result, our pursuit of Him has drifted into something more akin to placidity.

And yet, God redeemed us not simply to shift us at a later point to our eternal location, but also to introduce us to Him on earth. To know God personally is life's greatest pursuit. There is no end to knowing Him. Even in eternity, Scripture tells us that knowing God will be our aim (John 17:3).

So the question on the floor as we tackle this topic together is,

"How bad do you want it?" How bad do you really want to know Him, my friend? Is He worth your time in the morning? Is He worth setting aside your alone time or project time to seek Him? Is He worth opening yourself up and allowing yourself to become vulnerable in His presence? Is it worthwhile to integrate Him into every aspect of your life? Do you want to know Him that badly, or are you satisfied with a hello or a wave in passing every once in a while?

TRUE HUNGER

Exodus 33 tells about a time when Moses wanted God badly. Moses had come to know God through many experiences and had become dissatisfied with a nibble here or there. He was hungry and wanted more. So he came to the Lord and made three requests of Him. We read about them in the following verses:

> I pray You, if I have found favor in Your sight, let me know Your ways that I may know You, so that I may find favor in Your sight (verse 13).

> If Your presence does not go with us, do not lead us up from here (verse 15).

> I pray You, show me Your glory! (verse 18).

These are the words of a hungry man. In the natural realm, when you find yourself getting hungry, you go and look for something to eat. You look for something that will satiate your cravings and satisfy your need. And if you get hungry enough, there will be no stopping you from raiding the refrigerator or the pantry. In fact, you'll even get up in the middle of the night to do so if need be. Or head out to a fast-food joint after dark. This is because true hunger demands a response. True hunger will force you to rearrange your priorities.

Moses was a man who was famished for God. He asked God over and over again to remain in close proximity to him so that he could get to know Him. He asked Him to reveal Himself. He practically begged God not to lead him anywhere where God would not also be. When you are hungry for someone, you want to be near them. You want to close the distance—no matter the cost.

What's more, Moses' hunger wasn't predicated on a lack of knowing God. This was the man who saw God in the burning bush. This is the man through whom God orchestrated the ten supernatural events against Pharaoh. At God's command, he held out a rod and opened up the Red Sea. This was a man who already knew God quite well.

They say that familiarity can breed contempt, but not when authenticity punctuates the relationship. Moses had spent so much time in God's presence that he knew full well that he was no good outside of it. He had discovered that knowing God was what mattered most.

See, Moses understood something we often miss. He understood that if God could do all that He had done in and through Moses up until that point, there was abundantly more to Him that he had not yet tapped. God had been good to Moses. In fact, He had been great to Moses. He had performed miracles and delivered him. But that was yesterday, and yesterday had only whetted the appetite.

Moses needed fresh wind and fire when he spoke up to the Lord and said, "I want to know You more!"

The sons of Korah said it this way: "As the deer pants for the water brooks, so my soul pants for You, O God. My soul thirsts for God, for the living God; when shall I come and appear before God?" (Psalm 42:1-2). Paul put it this way: "Whatever things were gain to me, those things I have counted as loss for the sake of Christ. More than that, I count all things to be loss in view of the surpassing value of knowing Christ Jesus my Lord...that I may know Him and the power of His resurrection and the fellowship of His sufferings" (Philippians 3:7-8,10).

Hunger for God isn't only about blessings and having Him act on your behalf. Moses, the psalmists, and Paul hungered to know God fully, even in "the fellowship of His sufferings." When people experience a shared suffering or mutual struggle, it often will draw them closer together. It creates a greater appreciation for one another on many levels, while developing a deeper intimacy.

In fact, the whole book of Job is about a man who went through a severe testing and trial but, in the end, marveled in his new experience of knowing God as the outcome of his suffering. It wasn't until he came to know and understand God more closely that he was able to turn from his complaints and questions to a posture of wonder and intimacy. We read in Job 42, "I have heard of You by the hearing of the ear; but now my eye sees You; therefore I retract, and I repent in dust and ashes" (verses 5-6).

Figuratively speaking, Job was saying that he had been to church, gone through the catechism, and attended all the Bible classes. He had heard about God through "the hearing of the ear," but it wasn't until he experienced mess in his life that God opened his eyes to see Him for who He truly is. It wasn't until then that Job really knew God. And when he came to know Him, he became humble in His presence.

There's something about the power and majesty of God that, when we are finally able to recognize it, produces wonder, awe, and gratitude—even in the midst of difficult situations. Job's life gives us insight into the reality that whatever troubles we may be facing, it might be God trying to create an awareness and hunger in us for Him. Because when circumstances get really bad in life, we can no longer feed ourselves. We need someone else to help us. Sometimes God lets us hit rock bottom so that we will discover He is the rock at the bottom.

TO KNOW GOD'S WAYS

Moses made a very instructive statement when he said, "Let me know Your ways that I may know You" (Exodus 33:13). To know God's ways is to know God. To know His ways is to be synced up with what He is doing, to be aligned with His will and rule. It is to be on the same page with God. See, you can't truly know someone if you don't even know what they are up to. But even though that is true about our relationship with God, many of us miss that. Instead, we make our prayers about us. We make our requests not so He will show us what He is up to and how we can join Him, but so we can have our own way.

But to know God is to know His ways. Because Moses knew

God intimately, God showed him His ways (Psalm 103:7). And as we looked at briefly in the last chapter, His ways are not our ways, and His thoughts are not our thoughts (Isaiah 55:8). Friend, we can't know God while going about our own way. Which is why so many prayers simply go unanswered, because we ask God to do something that is not His way of doing it. Our prayers should focus on finding out from God what He is doing, what His heart is on a matter, and how we can participate with Him in His plan.

If God is going one way and you are going the other way, the fact that you are praying, reading your Bible, talking to other Christians, and going to church means absolutely nothing. This is because He's way over on one side facing one direction, and you are way over on the other. When two people are going in opposite directions, it is challenging to remain in contact. So you can't ask God to bless what you're asking Him to bless if you don't even know that He's heading in that direction. Moses made it clear that the first step in knowing God is knowing His ways: His path, His direction, His plan.

All your spiritual efforts and exercises become a waste if you are not seeking His ways. It's like coming off a service road and onto the highway. When you do, you have to merge onto the highway. You can't get off the service road and just turn left. If you do, there will be a wreck. You have to go with the flow of traffic. When you are not in the flow with God, you will face difficulties that have the potential to undo you, because these difficulties will not stem from trials designed to strengthen you, but rather from the consequences of poor choices.

Knowing God's ways and His path and then merging into that

is the only way to lasting peace in this life. It is also the only way to productivity that stretches into eternity.

TO EXPERIENCE GOD'S PRESENCE

Moses took his request further than just knowing God's ways, though. He also asked for God's presence as he traveled God's path. In Exodus 33:15, Moses tells the Lord that if His presence does not go with them, he doesn't want to go. If God wasn't going, Moses wasn't going. Moses wasn't satisfied with a program. He wasn't content with public approval. He didn't seek out the applause of people. No, he wanted one thing and one thing only: the presence of God. Without proximity, nothing else mattered to Moses. He wasn't about to take a step without first being assured that God was going with him, even if it meant not entering the promised land.

Sometimes God will test us to see whether we want the blessing more than the one who blesses. Thus, one of the questions we need to ask ourselves is, "Am I in the presence of God?"

Moses knew that the wilderness and terrain up ahead of him was rough. But he'd rather be in a desert with God than in the promised land all alone. It's like saying to a loved one, "I'd rather be poor with you than rich without you," or, "I'd rather live in an apartment with you than in a house without you." People will do that when love is introduced into the equation. If someone wants a relationship with another person badly enough, they will adjust. People will move to entirely new locations for a relationship or change their name because the relationship calls for it. They do these things because their hunger for the presence of the other person overrides their own personal plans.

Moses knew that God was in charge. He knew that God's plans superseded his own. He knew that his best bet in life was to adjust to where God was going, what God was doing, and how God was doing it. He had learned firsthand that plagues require the supernatural and parting seas takes more than just a rod. Moses had discovered through experiencing God for himself that knowing God was the most important, strategic, and powerful thing he could and should do.

TO SEE GOD'S GLORY

Moses made a third request in the Exodus 33 passage—to see God's glory (verse 18).

Glory is the visible display of the invisible God. It's when God makes Himself seeable, when He manifests His deity and attributes. Moses wasn't content with just knowing God's ways and having God's presence; Moses wanted it all. He wanted to see God's glory— the fullest unveiling possible. He wanted the rawest, purest manifestation that God would allow him to have. And he wanted to experience it firsthand.

One of the great scourges of our day is pornography. It's addictive, particularly for men, because it takes what is legitimate (sexual desire) and twists it into something that is not legitimate. The problem with pornography is that the desire is built in. The enemy takes what God has created for good and turns it around for bad.

At the heart of pornography is this need to piggyback on the intimacy of others. In other words, the viewer gets their thrill by watching someone else's thrill. It is essentially experiencing someone else's intimacy. Fundamentally, to depend on pornography reveals a person's lack. Because if they had it going on like it ought to be going on in their marriage relationship, they wouldn't need to turn to someone else for satisfaction.

Far too many of us, though, are spiritual pornographers. We can't access our own intimacy with God, so we come to church in order to piggyback on the intimacy of others, whether it's the worship leaders, choir, other members, or the preacher. We seek to "feel" intimate with God when we really aren't. It reveals our own inadequacies when the closest we feel to God is in a group context with others who are close to Him.

Moses didn't want to have any of that. He wanted God's glory for himself. And he didn't want God to hold anything back. His was the cry of a hungry man who wasn't willing to settle. He wanted it all.

Are you satisfied with a sermon and song? If so, welcome to a world of pedantic meandering and nothingness. God has designed you for so much more. And until you uncover how to tap into all He has created you to explore, you will live with lack. It may not always be overtly apparent, but it will manifest itself in a multitude of ways.

God values Himself too much to be misused by His people. That's why He's not going to reveal Himself to those who don't really want to know Him. He'll let you live with the gaping hole in your soul for as long as you want to do so. He's not into wasting His time or playing hide-and-seek with you. God wants to know that you want to know Him. In other words, He will only give you as much of Himself as you really want to have (Philippians 3:12).

But when you do seek God fully, like Moses did, be prepared for His answer. As He told Moses in Exodus 33,

> I Myself will make all My goodness pass before you, and will proclaim the name of the LORD before you; and I will be gracious to whom I will be gracious, and will show compassion on whom I will show compassion...You cannot see My face, for no man can see Me and live!...Behold, there is a place by Me, and you shall stand there on the rock; and it will come about, while My glory is passing by, that I will put you in the cleft of the rock and cover you with My hand until I have passed by. Then I will take My hand away and you shall see My back, but My face shall not be seen (verses 19-23).

God gave Moses his desire. He let His essence pass before Moses. And He protected him in the process as well, not displaying the full manifestation of His being, because that would have destroyed Moses. Like a nuclear reactor, the energy alone would have disintegrated him. So God put a rock and His hand between Himself and Moses so that Moses could experience as much of God as his human body had the capacity to experience.

It's like when an airplane flies in the sky above you, and you don't really see the airplane itself, but you see the contrail it leaves behind. God's energy is stronger than the sun which He created. For Moses to see anything but God's contrail would undo him. Yet because

Moses was hungry for God, God gave him a personal glimpse of Himself—as much as He could allow for Moses' sake.

Do you know what happened because Moses experienced God? He wrote, "In the beginning God created the heavens and the earth" (Genesis 1:1). And he kept going. God's presence empowered him with information he never could have gotten on his own. Moses penned the first five books of the Bible, even though he wasn't there to personally experience all the events. This is because God gave him backward revelation into the history and being of God.

Do you want insight into God's ways and His workings in your life and in the lives of those you love? Then seek God. Get to know Him. "Just as it is written, 'Things which eye has not seen and ear has not heard, and which have not entered the heart of man, all that God has prepared for those who love Him'" (1 Corinthians 2:9). Knowing God opens up a wealth of knowledge into all areas of life itself.

Do you want to know your calling? Then search after God, because He's the one who made it. Do you want to know what decision you should make on a certain issue? Look for God, because He knows the path you should take. Do you want to know how to be a better spouse, parent, or employee? Chase after God, because He knows how you should live.

The pursuit of God is not an ethereal, cloud-nine visit to never-never land as you play the harp and sing songs. No, the pursuit of knowing and understanding God unlocks all you need to fully live out the victorious kingdom life you were made to fulfill.

But one question remains: How bad do you want it?

3

MEETING GOD
FACE TO FACE

Back before seat belts, you could always tell when a couple was happy. Happy couples sat together on the driver's side of the car, cuddled up nearly as one. But when couples weren't happy, one person would be on the passenger's side, close to the door, and the other on the driver's side.

As the story goes, one day a husband and wife were driving, and the wife looked over to her husband and said, "We used to sit so close together."

To which the husband replied, "Well, I haven't moved."

If it feels like God is distant, He isn't the one who has moved. It simply means you have moved away from Him.

In Exodus 32, Israel experienced a breakdown in their relationship with God. They made choices which moved them further away from God.

If you are familiar with this story, you will recall that following their miraculous deliverance from slavery, the Israelites built themselves a golden calf to worship. This occurred after they had learned that God had said not to create any idols (Exodus 20:4-5), even if the idol is made with Him in mind.

Yet the Israelites grew frustrated when their leader, Moses, took too long to come back from spending time with God on the mountain. They felt alone. And we all know what happens when you feel alone. It ushers in feelings of helplessness and desperation. The Israelites felt their vulnerability immensely and sought to create something they could touch, see, feel, and have with them at all times.

When God saw what they had done, He became incensed. He was aggravated that the Israelites had so quickly and easily removed themselves from Him by committing this great and terrible sin. Thus, in Exodus 33:3 God told Moses, "Go up to a land flowing with milk and honey; for I will not go up in your midst, because you are an obstinate people, and I might destroy you on the way." That's an interesting statement. He literally told His people to go to the place of blessing, but He would not go with them. The land flowing with milk and honey was their dream, their goal. Evidently it is possible to be physically blessed, yet not have God with you. You can have circumstances going well for you but still be alone.

That's why you cannot look around you at what other people have or what other people are doing and assume they are close to God. Having a blessing does not reveal where someone stands with God in their personal relationship with Him. This principle is laid out for us in Matthew 5:45, which states, "He causes His sun to rise on the evil and the good, and sends rain on the righteous and the unrighteous."

Far too often, people look to the blessing as a validation of God's presence. But when we examine the lives of those in Scripture who were closest to God, we find tribulation, difficulties, and troubles. Being blessed is a wonderful thing, but it is not necessarily an indicator of a person's intimacy with the Lord. Remember, even Satan offered to bless Jesus (Luke 4:5-6). Unfortunately, it is far too easy to assume closeness based on tangible goods alone, which can lead to a level of apathy that stalls the pursuit of God in a believer's life.

God is not a piece of data. Knowing Him isn't akin to knowing how to play a game or manipulate something for your own good. Knowing God is an intense experience that plumbs the very depths of being. It's not about receiving spiritual serendipities or throwing out theological truths that sound good or make you seem like you know Him. Nor is it about amassing spiritual trophies or creating large platforms. Knowing God means sharing a personal relationship with Him.

THE TENT OF MEETING

Communicating with God is what Moses did in response to the Lord's anger toward the Israelites. Moses didn't erect a town hall and call for a public display of God's presence. No, he did what he always did. He sought God on God's terms, away from the fanfare of everyday life. He sought the Lord face to face, as he had done so many times before.

We read about this experience in Exodus 33:7-11, which sets the stage for our own discovery of how to know the Lord more deeply.

> Now Moses used to take the tent and pitch it out-side the camp, a good distance from the camp, and he called it the tent of meeting. And everyone who sought the LORD would go out to the tent of meeting which was outside the camp. And it came about, whenever Moses went out to the tent, that all the people would arise and stand, each at the entrance of his tent, and gaze after Moses until he entered the tent. When-ever Moses entered the tent, the pillar of cloud would descend and stand at the entrance of the tent; and the LORD would speak with Moses. When all the people saw the pillar of cloud standing at the entrance of the tent, all the people would arise and worship, each at the entrance of his tent. Thus the LORD used to speak to Moses face to face, just as a man speaks to his friend.

In the course of time, after the deliverance from the Egyptians, Moses had set up a tent called "the tent of meeting." This was a spe-cial tent with a special purpose. The purpose is given to us in verse 7; if a person wished to inquire of the Lord or to consult with God, this would serve as the location for doing so. We also see in verse 7 that this tent was situated "a good distance from the camp." In other words, the tent of meeting was not inside the camp. It was separate from the masses.

Why? Because this was a unique, holy place where people went when they really wanted to meet with God. This required a leaving of the ordinary, routine scenarios of life as they made their way to an extraordinary, set-apart place. Not only that, but we saw earlier in Exodus 33 that God was no longer dealing with His people inside the camp due to their sin and idolatry. He had already indicated that He would not be with them collectively at this time, but He was still making Himself personally available to those who demonstrated that they truly wanted to know Him.

What we uncover from this setup is that Moses would get away from the crowd and the everydayness of life in order to seek God. He would remove himself from the regular programming in order to focus entirely on God.

Have you ever spent time with someone who continues to pick up their phone to surf social media or just browse the internet? How does that make you feel? Or have you ever done that when you were with someone? Regardless of who is doing it, it sends a clear message that the person on the phone is not focusing on the other person. Their attention is divided at best or removed entirely at worst.

But consider how you feel when you set out to spend time with someone you care about, and they make it a point to say, "See this phone? I'm turning it off so that I can focus entirely on you and what we are doing right now." That action no doubt causes you to feel cherished, valued, and loved.

What God wants from us is much more than a nod, salute, or

high five when we walk by. He doesn't want a glance or a simple pause as we go about our day. While those things are nice, they cannot serve as the foundation for your relationship with God. He desires—and deserves—your full attention, effort, and focus. After all, what would have happened if He only halfheartedly threw together the universe? None of us would probably be here if that had been His approach. But God intricately wove each of us together and gave us a destiny (Psalm 139:13; Jeremiah 1:5). The least He'd like in return is a bit of focus on Him—a bit of devotion to Him.

When Moses met with God, Scripture tells us that a glory cloud (representing the presence of God) would descend upon the tent. The atmosphere literally reflected what was happening in and around Moses. But Moses only received this glory because he knew to take the time and make the effort to seek God on His turf.

One of the problems we have in our Christian walk today is that we do not meet God face to face, simply because we do not carve out the intentionality necessary to do so. Sure, we'll log on to an app here or pull up a devotional there—but that's not a tent of meeting. It's good, but it's not seeking out the dedicated, devoted place where it's just you and the Lord, face to face.

Taking time away from the everydayness of life requires planning and sacrifice. I understand that. Trust me, I do. Not only do I preach twice a week, but I also travel regularly to preach and serve as the president of our national ministry. On top of that, our family has been blessed with grandchildren galore who, thankfully, all live nearby. Needless to say, my life—and my schedule—is full. Probably just like it is for you.

But taking time out from my scheduled activities solely for the purpose of spending time in God's presence, at His altar, in His glory is my priority. It has to be. There's no way I can successfully keep up my schedule in my own human efforts. That's why you will find me in the early hours of the morning hanging out with my best friend, my confidant, my ruler, my God. Skipping those times with Him is detrimental in every area of my life. He's just too important, too critical, too needed. Just as He is too needed by you to be neglected. Scripture makes a big deal about the joy of seeking God in the morning (Psalm 92:1-2; 143:8; Mark 1:35).

But maybe you don't feel like you have the time. Or maybe you aren't a "morning person," per se. But if it's important enough to you, if it's critical for your direction in life, your schedule can be adjusted. People get up earlier when it really matters that they make it somewhere on time. If something is significant enough to you, you'll find the time. We all do.

Not too long ago I received a phone call from former president George W. Bush. He lives here in Dallas and just wanted to get together for lunch. Now, like I said, I keep a fairly tight schedule—often established a year in advance—but when the former president of the United States calls you and asks if you can have lunch with him next week (even if it's on a Tuesday, which is my busiest day of the week!), you find the time.

I found the time.

And friend, I know that if you value knowing God at the level He desires you to value that pursuit, you will find the time as well.

FACE TIME

As we dive deeper into what it means to pursue intimacy with the Lord, I understand that you may be thinking about how different things are today from how they were in the days of the Bible. It seems that in the Jewish culture of the Old Testament, prophets and people heard from God in a more straightforward fashion than we do today. That's not the case, but it does seem like that sometimes. One of the problems we face with hearing God is that we simply have too much noise on the line. We have too much clutter in the atmosphere. We have become too easily distracted by things that matter little—or even matter not.

Consider the story of a Native American who was walking down the street one day in the bustling city of New York. Crowds of feet hit the pavement like hail in a summer storm. An American businessman walked beside him.

"Did you hear that?" the Native American asked his friend.

"Hear what?" his friend replied, confused by the question, especially in the midst of so much noise.

"The cricket. Did you hear the cricket?" the Native American replied.

The businessman shrugged his shoulders and then laughed. No way did he hear a cricket. Surely his friend was joking.

"No, there really is a cricket," the Native American replied. Then he took some time to trace the sound until he spotted the cricket. Showing his friend, he smiled knowingly.

"How in the world did you hear that cricket?" the man asked.

"It's simple," came the reply. Then the Native American reached into his pocket, pulled out some coins, and dropped them on the pavement. Heads turned. Eyes darted. And people who had moments earlier appeared to be oblivious to their surroundings went to pick up the coins.

"You hear what you're listening for," said the Native American to his friend. "See?"

It's true. A mother can hear the faint tossing and turning or mumblings from her infant in a room down the hall, out of earshot of most people. This is because a mother's ears have been trained to listen to the needs and calls of her baby.

A hunter can hear the quiet steps of a deer pausing to see if anything is on its tail. And an entire line of bent-over soldiers with helmets on, encompassed by the screams of large crowds, can hear the voice of the one man who is telling them what to do. We hear what we want to hear. So if you are not hearing God talking to you, it is probably because you have not trained your ears to recognize His voice.

Once you learn how to tune in to the Spirit's still, small voice speaking into your heart, thoughts, and very spirit, you will discover that God speaks far more often than you ever imagined. Sometimes He's funny. Other times He's compassionate. There are times when He's serious, guiding or correcting you. And, like any parent, there are also times when He delights in you or something you've done. God is the most multifaceted, emotional being in existence. Yet so many of us never come to know Him in a way that allows us to see Him for who He truly is.

God is not some stuffy old man in a tight suit with a scowl on

His face, sitting on clouds and waiting to shoot someone with lightning. Nor is He a cosmic Santa Claus with a big belly and jolly grin. Rather, God envelops and embodies every creative design, every passion, and every dreamer's vision—all within the context of His sinless self.

If you want to know how beautiful He is, take a moment to look at the ocean waves rolling in over the seashore. If you want to know how grand He is, glance at a mountain stretching into the sky. If you want to know how compassionate He is, spend some time thinking through your sins and how He has blessed you by forgiving you and granting you a new start time and again because of the sacrificial death of His Son.

God is more artistic than the most famous painter or musician to ever live. He has so much to tell you if you will learn to listen to Him. He has so much to share with you if you will seek Him outside the camp, beyond empty religion.

Never be satisfied with worshiping God from a distance. We saw in the Exodus 33 passage that the Israelites stayed by their own tents when Moses went to the tent of meeting. Apparently they were satisfied with the passenger's side of the car. They were satisfied with a Sunday morning service once a week or a small group gathering on Tuesdays. But not Moses. Moses wanted more. "Thus the LORD used to speak to Moses face to face, just as a man speaks to his friend" (verse 11).

Do you desire to have God speak to you face to face—openly and honestly, with a free flow of communication? Then start to speak to Him the same way.

One of the ways you can know that a person is not as close to God as they may "sound" is that they relate to God in the abstract. Their prayers reside in ethereal terms such as, "Oh Father, Creator of heaven and earth, awesome designer of the universe, the unseen hand..." While it is good to acknowledge God's power and might, it is not indicative of intimacy if that's the only way a person speaks to God. No, that illustrates a relationship based more on form and process than on friendship and pairing.

Another way you can tell when a person is not as close to God as they may "sound" is when their prayers merely repeat the same words over and over and over again *ad nauseam.* "Bless me; bless my children; bless my job; etc." Do you know how well a relationship with a friend would turn out if that's how you chose to communicate with that friend? Not very well at all.

Friends talk about everything. There is an exposure of being that informs the conversation. In other words, when husbands and wives sit down with each other and no longer have anything to say, that means that something negative is happening in the relationship. They are duty bound to spend time together, but a lack of relational intimacy reveals itself in a lack of free-flowing communication.

Talking freely with God goes further than saying, "Lord, forgive me of my sins." When you talk face to face with the Lord, you tell Him the specific sins you are struggling with, what happened that day, what you thought, what you want to do that you shouldn't, and so on. He knows what you are thinking, doing, saying, and struggling with anyhow. You're not keeping it hidden by not telling Him. Face-to-face conversation is open and honest conversation.

You will never experience God until you are willing to regularly speak openly with Him. If you stay vague, He'll stay vague. If that's all you want, that's all He'll give you. He's not going to force Himself upon you. He wants to be your friend.

A close friend is like the best man or maid of honor at a wedding, not just someone in attendance. They are that special person you know you can count on when life gets you down. They are the first person who comes to mind when something great happens and you want to share about it. This kind of friend never leaves your side, and you never want to leave theirs either. That's the kind of relationship the Lord longs to have with you. He wants all of you. He is a jealous God who does not wish to share you.

James 4:4 tells us, "Do you not know that friendship with the world is hostility toward God? Therefore whoever wishes to be a friend of the world makes himself an enemy of God." Thus, if you are still more committed to the camp or your own tent than to seeking God outside the everydayness of life, then you have chosen friendship with the world over Him.

Yes, you are supposed to live in this world—just not be of it. This is similar to how a boat is on the water, but the water is not in the boat. When the water gets in the boat, it causes all kinds of problems. Some of us are too tied to the world to go meet with God. Or we don't want the rejection that comes from being too committed to God. But even Christ subjected Himself to that rejection by purchasing our redemption outside the camp, as we read in Hebrews 13:12-14.

> Jesus also, that He might sanctify the people through
> His own blood, suffered outside the gate. So, let us go

out to Him outside the camp, bearing His reproach.
For here we do not have a lasting city, but we are seeking the city which is to come.

God is the consummate gentleman. If you want to be more committed to the world than to Him, He won't berate you. But you
won't get more of Him. And not to have the full experience God has
to offer of Himself on this side of heaven is to miss the very essence
of why we were created. We were made for Him. Which is why He
has taken the time in His Word to instruct us again and again on
how to know Him. He is inviting us to a special place, away from
the distractions of life. A place where we will get answers from Him.
A place where we will find refreshment in Him. A place where we
will grow, laugh, love, and find lasting peace. It's all there, in Him.

Many of us, in the span of our lives, have been on blind dates.
Going on a blind date usually means you got some information,
but you have yet to experience a face-to-face meeting. Someone has
told you good things about the person, but until you actually meet,
you don't know for sure if it's true. The information you receive
increases your appetite to know more, but it doesn't actually cause
you to know more. You can only know more when you spend time
together.

God has given us more than enough information to increase our
appetites for Him. But unless we take the step to actually meet with
Him, we'll be living with information about Him and nothing more.

To know God more deeply as you continue this quest into
exploring His depths, start by identifying your "tent of meeting."
This is the place you will go to spend undistracted time with Him

for extended amounts of time. This is not a quick five-minute devotion you do before you run out of the house and start your day. No,
this is abiding, hanging out—getting to know Him.

If you lack or have lost the desire to put this practice into motion,
I recommend that you surround yourself with people who have an
appetite for God. If you're not hungry, then go somewhere where
they cook great food. The smells alone will entice you to take a bite
or two.

When a person is hospitalized and can no longer eat, the doctors
know that they need to insert a feeding tube, or the patient will die.
Likewise, if you are in a spiritual ICU and just don't know how to
make seeking God a priority, give Him permission to feed you until
your spiritual health returns.

Make it a priority to meet with God regularly, even if it's just for
a short amount of time, and allow those times to grow as you come
to recognize His voice more and more each day. Pray simply, "Lord,
I want to know You. Show me Your glory." Then open your eyes
and buckle your seat belt, because that is a prayer He will gladly
answer for you.

4

TRANSFORMED IN GOD'S PRESENCE

Over the course of the last few years, I've taken a steady, consistent approach to weight loss. I haven't gone on a crash diet. I haven't become obsessed with exercise. I haven't denied myself portions of the food I love—like fried chicken or doughnuts or my wife's home cooking. But I have limited those portions to a more reasonable amount and increased my exercise.

My weight loss hasn't come quickly, but it has come regularly. In these last few years, I have reached my doctor's goal for what he considered to be a more advantageous weight for my age and body type.

As a result, I feel better. I have more energy. And I get to hear a lot of nice comments from people who have taken notice!

But there was a show on television which featured people pursuing weight loss who struggled in this arena at a much more aggressive level. It was called *The Biggest Loser*. On this show, 12 contestants would compete by participating in a rigid exercise program and strict eating schedule overseen by fitness trainers and nutritionists. For the contestants, the transformation seemed to come almost overnight. Pounds melted away and clothes got swapped nearly weekly.

The average weight loss for 14 contestants who did the 30-week program was 130 pounds. That's more than four pounds a week![2] You can imagine the physical difference when someone loses that much weight. The transformation is visible. Similarly, when we undergo a spiritual transformation by practicing the presence of God, it ought to be recognizable not only to ourselves, but also to others.

Which brings me to some questions for us to consider in this chapter:

- How do you know when you are truly getting to know God and being transformed by Him?
- How do you know when spending time with Him is making a difference?
- How do you know when you are indeed establishing a personal, intimate relationship with Him?

You know because you are changing. You are changing in a way that involves your character, words, decisions, and drive. You are changing in a way that is demonstrable to those around you. They can see it.

Change is important. Progression in our transformation is necessary. We live in a quantifiable, measurable culture. Analytics, benchmarks, and goals often drive us. The bottom line dictates our decisions. And as you get to know God, you should experience a noticeable life change. Essentially, the proof that you are getting to know God more intimately and personally is that you are transformed both internally and externally. Thus, if you are not changing, you are not getting to know God. Rather, you have adopted a program, plan, thesis, or theory instead of a personal pursuit of Him.

Knowing God has nothing to do with how many ministries you serve in, how much money you give, or how many prayers you say. All those things have their place, but if you are not being transformed as an individual, knowing God is not on the table.

Many people feel as if the idea of getting to know God involves some ethereal, metaphysical meditation. And while there certainly is a spiritual component to experiencing His presence, there are also tangible results.

Let me ask you this: How do you know when a child is growing? I can imagine your answer: Because the child is changing. The child starts as a little baby, then starts crawling, standing, walking, and even running at some point. There is change with physical growth—visible transformation. If a two-year-old can still fit in an infant onesie, that's an indication that something is wrong. In fact, the moment a child stops growing is when the doctor takes notice and starts looking for what may be causing the problem.

Similarly, as you grow in your relationship with the living, holy, all-powerful God, you will also change. As your soul absorbs more of His Spirit, you will change. As His thoughts become more prominent in your thoughts, you will change. As His will comes to dominate your will, you will change.

If you are not changing in your character, conduct, attitudes, and actions, you are not growing in your knowing of God. It's as straightforward as that.

MOSES ON THE MOUNTAIN

In Exodus 34, we come across a scene somewhat reminiscent of Moses and the burning bush, in that he was on a mountain, encountering the Lord. Scripture informs us that Moses was there fasting 40 days and 40 nights, not eating or drinking (verse 28). In this season of surrender, God spoke to Moses. We read, "The LORD said to Moses, 'Write down these words, for in accordance with these words I have made a covenant with you and with Israel'" (verse 27). And God gave the Ten Commandments to Moses.

While this reflects the part of the exchange we tend to focus on, what happened next is just as important in revealing to us what happens when we truly know God. Verses 29-30 say,

> It came about when Moses was coming down from Mount Sinai (and the two tablets of the testimony were in Moses' hand as he was coming down from the mountain), that Moses did not know that the skin of his face shone because of his speaking with Him. So when Aaron and all the sons of Israel saw Moses,

behold, the skin of his face shone, and they were afraid
to come near him.

Like somebody spending time in a nuclear reactor, Moses' skin
showed the effects of being close to unlimited power and radiance.
God's presence had so rubbed off on Moses that his face literally
shone. His extended, uninterrupted time with the Lord transformed not only what he did, but also how he appeared. It transformed him in a recognizable manner.

Bear in mind, Moses was not satisfied with a quick visit to
the tent outside the camp. He sought a habitation. He sacrificed
physical pleasure (food and drink) for spiritual sanctity. He spent
extended, intentional time in God's presence.

Which makes me wonder how much of our days are spent like
that. Most of us pay God a quick visit, like a drop-in on a shut-in.
We give Him pleasantries and a bit of our attention, letting Him
know that we remember where He lives, but that's about it. And
yet, we complain that God does not show up in our chaos, mess, or
misery like we want Him to.

But there is a pattern to receiving the power of God's presence,
which is presented to us in this scene of Moses on the mountain.
It begins with Moses pursuing God outside the normal routine of
life. Then he gave up the physical pleasures of this life—comfort,
food, and even safety. Then he received God's Word (the Ten Commandments). Through the process, Moses' life (inside and out) were
transformed.

What is most interesting about this, though, is that other people noticed the change before Moses even did. He was so caught up

in the experience itself that he lost track of the personal outcome. As we read in Exodus 34:30, Aaron and the sons of Israel saw that Moses' face shone and became afraid. Moses had to call out to them and ask them to set aside their fears and come near him (verses 31-32). The Israelites had noticed Moses' time spent with God.

Have you ever seen a woman who has fallen deeply in love? She doesn't even have to tell you. Why? Because her face is glowing. She radiates the energy of the love she feels inside. This is because she's been in the presence of a man who has affected her. In fact, you can often tell the temperature of a marriage based on a woman's glow. If her face looks sullen and her eyes look dim, that reveals a lot about the warmth of her relationship. The quality of love impacts a person's interior and exterior.

Which is why when you get to know God on a personal, deep level and experience more of His grace, glory, and love in your life, it will show through your demeanor and countenance. What God is after in His relationship with you is total transformation of your heart, mind, spirit, and even your body in some ways. He wants you to reflect Him in such a manner that invites others to know Him more.

Friend, that kind of transformation only comes through God. You can't get it just through hearing a Sunday morning sermon. You can't even get it by blasting worship songs in your home or car. While these things can inform, encourage, and inspire you, they (in and of themselves) will not transform you. It is the job of the Holy Spirit to transform you in the abiding, lasting presence of God.

When you listen to a sermon and get all enthusiastic about your spiritual life as a result, that enthusiasm begins to wane—sometimes as soon as you walk out the church door. This is because you can't take the sermon with you. Yes, you may have jotted down some notes to review at a later time, but you'll never quite revive the experience of the moment simply because the experience itself is over.

Or if you listen to a worship song and feel lifted up into the clouds of heaven, as soon as the song is over—or when the children interrupt your thoughts with a need, or you get a phone call, etc.—that experience transitions into something else. And while you may carry a residual feeling of joy with you, that will also pass.

The only true way to remain connected with the power of knowing God is through God Himself. And He has made that way possible through the death, burial, and resurrection of His Son, Jesus Christ. It was through Christ's death that the pathway for the Holy Spirit's ongoing dwelling within us was made available.

Moses had to go to a mountain to spend time in proximity with God. But we don't need to do that today. By the grace of God supplied through Christ, we have the capacity and opportunity to remain in close proximity with God throughout every moment of every day, no matter where we are, what we are doing, or what distractions may surround us. This is because we have access to God at any time.

The Holy Spirit provides this proximity through His presence within us. Time and again we read of this placement of God's presence in us:

> If the Spirit of Him who raised Jesus from the dead
> dwells in you, He who raised Christ Jesus from the

dead will also give life to your mortal bodies through His Spirit who dwells in you (Romans 8:11).

Do you not know that you are a temple of God and that the Spirit of God dwells in you? (1 Corinthians 3:16).

Guard, through the Holy Spirit who dwells in us, the treasure which has been entrusted to you (2 Timothy 1:14).

When He, the Spirit of truth, comes, He will guide you into all the truth; for He will not speak on His own initiative, but whatever He hears, He will speak; and He will disclose to you what is to come (John 16:13).

As for you, the anointing which you received from Him abides in you, and you have no need for anyone to teach you; but as His anointing teaches you about all things, and is true and is not a lie, and just as it has taught you, you abide in Him (1 John 2:27).

As you can see from these passages (and many others throughout the Bible), the Spirit's role involves guiding, teaching, comforting, and providing access to God. We have no excuse in today's age for not growing close to God. He has made Himself available to us in every way.

God so desires for you to draw near to Him that He sacrificed His Son to give you that opportunity. He wants you to give Him the freedom to rub off on you. He desires to both affect and infect you with His presence. When He does, you will experience a transformation like none other. His thinking will start to become your thinking. His feelings will start to become your feelings. His reactions will start to become your reactions. His attitudes will start to become your attitudes.

It's more than a glow or some other visual reflection of closeness. When you come to know God for yourself at a deep, penetrating level, He transforms your thoughts, desires, decisions, and actions.

FROM GLORY TO GLORY

Drawing close to God no longer requires scaling a mountain or taking a solitary trek into the wilderness. Drawing close to God occurs internally through an abiding relationship with Him. Paul instructs us on how this happens when he writes about Moses and the glory he experienced on the mountain. Lest you think that what Moses had was greater than what we have access to today, Paul pens clearly that we are even better positioned toward proximity with God than during Moses' time in the Old Testament. We read,

> You are a letter of Christ, cared for by us, written not with ink but with the Spirit of the living God, not on tablets of stone but on tablets of human hearts.

> Such confidence we have through Christ toward God. Not that we are adequate in ourselves to consider anything as coming from ourselves, but our adequacy is from God, who also made us adequate as servants of a new covenant, not of the letter but of the Spirit; for the letter kills, but the Spirit gives life.

But if the ministry of death, in letters engraved on stones, came with glory, so that the sons of Israel could not look intently at the face of Moses because of the glory of his face, fading as it was, how will the ministry of the Spirit fail to be even more with glory? For if the ministry of condemnation has glory, much more does the ministry of righteousness abound in glory. For indeed what had glory, in this case has no glory because of the glory that surpasses it. For if that which fades away was with glory, much more that which remains is in glory (2 Corinthians 3:3-11).

Paul points out that although what Moses had was considered great in his day, it is not a representation of what we have today. After all, the Ten Commandments given to Moses by God carried with them condemnation. Paul refers to them as "the ministry of death." When you read through the Ten Commandments, you'll notice the repetitive pattern of "Thou shalt not" (Exodus 20 KJV). And if those who lived by these commandments failed to abide by them, they would face repercussions—severe ones at that.

In pointing out that what Moses received, involving a message of consequences and condemnation when violated, came with glory, Paul urges us to recognize how much more of the glory of God is available through the message of Christ. In other words, if Moses could go up a mountain and get negative, condemnatory information from God and still manage to come down with the glow of God's glory, then what we have access to today greatly surpasses that.

Paul also reminds us that the further Moses went from God and the closer he got to his own people, the more the glory he had received began to fade. This is similar to what I mentioned earlier about the spiritual passion you often feel in relation to a sermon or song. It can lift your spirit when the service, the choir, or the preacher is on fire. It feels as if God is literally all over you.

But the more time removes you from the actual experience of the sermon or song, the inspiration also dwindles. By the time you reach your car in the church parking lot, that glory can fade away in light of life's realities. And you might start to wonder why you even bother coming to church at all—or the people riding with you in the car might wonder that about you!

It's not that the spiritual experience wasn't glorious in the moment; it's just that it is fading. Like what happened with Moses, the glory diminishes as you go back to dealing with people.

But what Paul wants us to know is that what we have access to today is an ever-increasing glory. In fact, he tells us that the ministry of righteousness abounds in glory and surpasses the glory Moses experienced to such an extent that such glory is no glory at all (2 Corinthians 3:9-10). This is because the presence of God through the indwelling righteousness of the Holy Spirit, purchased through the blood of Jesus Christ, is available at all times. It does not have to fade because He is personally with us always.

However, just because God is with us in close proximity at all times does not mean that each of us accesses and experiences Him fully. Paul explains why this occurs in verses 12-16.

> Having such a hope, we use great boldness in our speech,
> and are not like Moses, who used to put a veil over his
> face so that the sons of Israel would not look intently at

the end of what was fading away. But their minds were
hardened; for until this very day at the reading of the
old covenant the same veil remains unlifted, because it
is removed in Christ. But to this day whenever Moses
is read, a veil lies over their heart; but whenever a person turns to the Lord, the veil is taken away.

The best way I know to illustrate this truth is to consider a wedding. While it doesn't take place at every wedding today, in the past
a bride often wore a veil over her face. After she had prepared her-
self in all her glory, she would hide her beauty beneath this veil.
Attendees could see the beauty of her dress and the exquisite way she
walked down the aisle, but her face could not be fully seen by anyone until the veil was lifted in front of her husband. This lifting of
the veil provided her husband a uniquely personal look at her glory.

Similarly, Paul explains in the 2 Corinthians passage how Moses
placed a veil over his face so that the sons of Israel could not see the
glory he carried from spending time with the Lord. And yet, while
the veil over God's glory has since been lifted through the sacrifice
of Jesus Christ, a veil can remain over the hearts of those who are
not turned toward the Lord.

It is only in turning toward God that the veil is taken away.

It is only in pursuing His heart that the veil over your own heart
can be lifted.

And what are some of the benefits of having the veil lifted? Paul
shares with us in the next two verses:

Now the Lord is the Spirit, and where the Spirit of
the Lord is, there is liberty. But we all, with unveiled

face, beholding as in a mirror the glory of the Lord,
are being transformed into the same image from glory
to glory, just as from the Lord, the Spirit (2 Corinthians 3:17-18).

Did you catch that? One of the premier benefits of intimacy with
the Lord is liberty—freedom, victory, deliverance from illegitimate
bondage. We have access to the victorious Christian life by closely
abiding with God through His Spirit. This victory is ours as a natural outgrowth of our relationship with Him.

Not only do you and I have access, but every believer has access.
Notice that Paul pens, "We all..." (verse 18). Back in Moses' day, no
one else walked around with their face shining like he did. We don't
read about anyone else climbing the mountain and experiencing
God closely. Moses was unique; he was special. His experience was
limited to himself. Everyone else merely got to look on and observe
what God was doing with Moses.

Yet in our day, this is no longer the case. In the New Covenant,
each one of us has access to what Moses had. Closeness with God is
not limited to a Moses of our time. Nor is it limited to superhumans
or special Christians. God's transforming glory is available to us all.

That means if you are saved, you are not an exception. You can
know God just like the most spiritual person you know. That's
why you can't go around saying things like, "I wish I was similar to
Brother So-and-So or Sister So-and-So. They seem so close to God!"
You can't say that because you have just as much access to God as
anyone else. Whether or not you enter that area of access, though,
is up to you.

To enter it, you must come "with unveiled face." That means you must come without camouflage or covering. Far too often, our church pews and pulpits are lined with people who are inauthentic. Smiles camouflage pain. Hair veils grief. Laughter and hallelujahs cover up personal sin and struggle.

Truth be told, most of us attending church on Sunday paint life much rosier than it actually is. Perhaps our family is close to disaster, or our finances are on the verge of destruction, or we're experiencing a health issue, addiction, or just plain loneliness and emptiness. Whatever the hardship, many of us camouflage our crying with cuteness. And while that camouflage may help Sunday morning be more palatable to us, it does not help us in how we relate to God.

God says if you are to come to Him, you must come with unveiled face—no camouflage or covering allowed. You can't come praying like everything is all right when it's not all right. You can't come talking to God like you're okay when both you and God know you're not okay. You can't come with praises and pleasant-sounding words when that's not really in your heart. Nor can you come with general statements about nothingness when you are facing specific struggles.

To come to God with unveiled face, you have to remove all coverings and enter into His presence with the raw reality of who you are. God is not looking for a cute visit from you. He's not asking you to put on a suit and tie or skirt and blouse and get all dressed up for your time with Him. We hear Him say in His own words what matters most to Him:

> Do not look at his appearance or at the height of his stature, because I have rejected him; for God sees not

as man sees, for man looks at the outward appearance,
but the LORD looks at the heart (1 Samuel 16:7).

God desires authenticity, honesty, and humility. He's not search-ing for the best Instagram account with pictures that follow a brand-ing style but rarely reflect the truth behind the smiles. He already knows that truth, so He simply asks that you acknowledge it to Him as well—that you come clean before Him, stripped of all pretense, piety, and public façade.

And when you do, God promises to transform you. As we read earlier, "We all, with unveiled face, beholding as in a mirror the glory of the Lord, are being transformed into the same image from glory to glory" (2 Corinthians 3:18). What do you behold in the mirror when you look into it? You see the image of what is in front of the mirror, an identical reflection of what stands before it. Sim-ilarly, the Lord tells us that when we come to Him and His Word with unveiled face, His glory becomes our reflection. He literally transforms the barrenness and brokenness of who we are into the purity of His own image. He transforms us by His Spirit into "the image of His Son" (Romans 8:29). What's more, He transforms us "from glory to glory," from one level of transformation to another.

See, Moses went from glory to less glory. His glory faded.

But you are not like Moses.

God has given you access to know Him at such an intimate level that you can go from glory to more glory. What He offers you is an ever-increasing glory. It's yours for the asking when you intention-ally choose to turn toward God with unveiled face—meaning in both spirit and truth (John 4:24).

When you do, you will change. You won't have to try to change; you simply will.

Have you ever known someone who is battling a stronghold or seeking to overcome a habit, and they use phrases such as "I'm trying" or "I'm working on it"? Or maybe you've been that someone.

But what God tells us through the 2 Corinthians passage we've been studying is that change will come naturally, simply by spending time in His presence. In other words, the Lord will bring about the transformation. You will not need to try to force it yourself. The closer you grow toward God in authenticity and intentionality, the more He will change you into the likeness of His glory—until you reach the point where you can look at certain strongholds you have faced in your life or certain difficulties you have struggled to overcome and wonder why they no longer have the power over you that they used to have. And the reason is because as you are transformed into a reflection of God's glory, His Spirit combined with His Word will enable you to access His power and strength.

Knowing God is not some otherworldly experience meant only for monks tucked away on mountains. Knowing God is the entry point for a life filled with victory, freedom, and power. And friend, that victory, freedom, and power are closer than you've ever imagined.

5

THAT YOU MAY KNOW GOD

On any given Sunday, as I preach to a church full of several thousand people, inevitably a cry will arise from somewhere in the congregation. Actually, it would be an odd Sunday if it were only one cry; I usually hear the cries of several babies over the course of two services. Normally, I'll notice some stirring in the seats as people look around to see what the mom or dad is going to do. Sometimes one of the parents gets up and takes the crying infant out of the sanctuary. Other times the crying infant can be soothed enough to stop crying, typically with a pacifier.

But then there are those times when the crying infant is too hungry to be soothed by a pacifier, which provides only a bit of calm before the crisis. This is because a pacifier is fundamentally a lie. It is designed to give the impression that the baby is being fed when they are not. It is an artificial replacement of the real thing, designed to keep the baby at bay until the service is over.

While a pacifier does often quiet a baby at first, after a while the baby will wise up. And when the baby wises up, it becomes clear to everyone in the sanctuary that there is no milk in that pacifier.

Many people come to church Sunday after Sunday to be pacified. They want enough to make them feel like they've gotten something, only to discover all week long that they are still hungry. So they show up again on Wednesday night or at a small group gathering or at the next Sunday service to get more pacification. They look for it in a service, song, or sermon, only to wise up to the hunger still within them. Sure, they get something that gives them the impression of the real thing, but they soon realize that something else is still miss-ing. They do not sense the nutritional value that they'd expected to have passed on to them.

As we continue our study on intimately knowing God, I'd like to suggest something to you: As long as you are satisfied with pac-ifiers, you won't cry out for the real thing. As long as you can get by on what is not real because it tides you over until the next time, your experience won't ever get real. Unless you become like the baby who rejects pacification—the religious, ritualistic ceremony of going through the motions—you will never find the true nour-ishment that comes from knowing God experientially. The real question I've been asking all along is this: How hungry are you to know God? Because God feeds those who cry out in hunger for Him.

OF SURPASSING VALUE

One of the hungriest people in Scripture was the apostle Paul. From a prison cell, where he no doubt suffered deprivation and pain, he penned some of the most profound insights in all recorded history. His letter was written to the church at Philippi, but the principles within the book apply to us today just as much as they did back then.

In chapter 3 of this letter, Paul wrote,

> Whatever things were gain to me, those things I have counted as loss for the sake of Christ. More than that, I count all things to be loss in view of the surpassing value of knowing Christ Jesus my Lord, for whom I have suffered the loss of all things, and count them but rubbish so that I may gain Christ (verses 7-8).

You can tell a lot about a person when they are at their lowest point. Whether it's a health crisis, financial disaster, or relational issues, what matters most usually rises to the surface when life boils over. Here was Paul struggling in a scenario that gave him no creature comforts, no relational intimacy, no financial stability, and no personal security. Yet, in the midst of his most dire situation, he wrote about things like value and gain—not tied to an IRA or platform, but tied to knowing Jesus Christ.

Paul was hungry for more than just food. In fact, he was so

hungry to know Christ that he said nothing else mattered to him anymore except for that. Although his circumstances were negative, they did not control his well-being. Paul had an inner contentment in knowing that the greatest pursuit in life—that of knowing God (through His Son, Jesus Christ)—was his highest aim.

Hebrews 1:3 tells us that Jesus Christ manifested the invisible as the visible: "He is the radiance of His glory and the exact representation of His nature, and upholds all things by the word of His power." We also see this in John 1:18, which says, "No one has seen God at any time; the only begotten God who is in the bosom of the Father, He has explained Him." To put it in everyday language, Jesus is God's selfie. God became a man so that as you relate to Jesus, you come to know God. Jesus is our pathway to the Father.

The story is told of a soldier sitting outside the White House one day, crying uncontrollably. A little boy saw him weeping and asked, "Sir, what's wrong?"

The soldier replied, "I was hoping I could see President Lincoln. We've got this devastating situation, and only the president can intervene and save the lives of my men. But they won't let me in."

The little boy took the soldier's hand and said, "Come with me."

They then proceeded to walk past the sentry at the gate and straight into the White House, past the guards. They then walked right into the president's office, and the little boy said, "Dad, this soldier needs to talk with you."

Sometimes it may feel like you can't get to God. You can't see Him, feel Him, touch Him. It seems as if He is this cosmic being far off in never-never land. But it is through the life of Jesus Christ, who came to earth as a human and who understands your weaknesses and struggles (Hebrews 4:15-16), that you have full access to the Father. Jesus offers His hand and says, "Come with me, you who are weary and burdened. I know exactly where to lead you" (see Matthew 11:28).

No doubt Paul was weary. No doubt he was burdened. But he had learned what most of us do not yet know—that there is greater value in knowing God than in anything that produces momentary pleasure. It wasn't because Paul had never known greatness, accomplishment, or achievement that he chose contentment so readily. Paul had been very successful in his culture, both in his pedigree and in power. In Philippians 3:4-6, he listed the things about which (from a human standpoint) he could boast. Paul had known luxury, power, and prestige. Yet here he sat dirty and hungry in a prison, saying none of that was worth even as much as rubbish when compared to the surpassing greatness of knowing Jesus Christ (verses 7-8).

Let me give you another word for what has been translated in verse 8 as *rubbish*—and that is *manure*. When was the last time you saw somebody studying manure, bragging on manure, or cherishing manure? If you saw someone doing those things, you would say that something was wrong with them. I would say the same thing, because that's waste.

Yet what Paul was saying is that you cannot gain Christ and cherish rubbish at the same time. Essentially, you can't cherish human achievement and gain the knowledge of Christ. You can't make a big deal out of the things that people make a big deal out of while simultaneously thinking that God is making a big deal out of it too.

Because He's not. Cherishing worldly success and knowing Christ are mutually exclusive activities.

Paul didn't say, "In addition to everything I have gained in life, including all the accomplishments, likes, followers, and sales I amassed, I'm also glad I know Christ." No, he said that he counted all of those things as a loss compared to the value of gaining an intimate knowledge of Jesus.

Yes, you may be great at your job or have an awesome personality or enormous bank account. But none of that will give you clout in heaven. None of that will give God a reason to applaud you. Don't misunderstand the underlying principle I'm seeking to emphasize. I'm not saying there is something wrong with achievement. Paul didn't say that either. What he did say is that when it comes to knowing God, those things are not the criteria God uses. What makes you big among men may actually make you small to God. Focusing on human notoriety, resources, or success is not akin to focusing on God.

What Paul wanted us to realize is that there is a treasure far more valuable than any offered by humanity. That's why his next statement reads, "May be found in Him, not having a righteousness of my own derived from the Law, but that which is through faith in Christ, the righteousness which comes from God on the basis of faith" (Philippians 3:9).

Paul made it clear that the standard by which he wanted to be measured was not one based on his own deeds or righteousness. Rather, he wanted to be measured solely on the righteousness imputed to him by virtue of faith in Jesus Christ. He desired this because he knew that self-righteousness was worth little more than "filthy rags" (Isaiah 64:6 KJV). He knew that the only perfect righteousness in existence is that which is deposited into every believer upon salvation. This righteousness, implanted within us in seed form as the Holy Spirit, produces Christ's righteousness as we grow in our sanctification through Him (1 Peter 1:23). As the Spirit of Christ develops a believer from within, that believer manifests the righteousness of Christ in word and action. It is the growth of the Spirit's rule over our own fleshly will and desires that produces the transformation. It is the growth of the Spirit's influence that enables us to shift our perspective on what is truly valuable.

FELLOWSHIP OF SUFFERING

So extreme is this shift when aligned with God's eternal mindset that we read of Paul's desire to share in the sufferings of Christ. Not only did Paul dismiss his own earthly gains and count them as loss, but he also intentionally pursued an understanding and experience of the loss, grief, pain, and shame that Jesus felt on earth. He wrote, "That I may know Him and the power of His resurrection and the fellowship of His sufferings, being conformed to His death" (Philippians 3:10).

Paul wasn't satisfied with an acquaintance with God. He had seen the power God held and wanted access to that power. This is the same power that got Jesus up from the grave. In order to pursue that power, Paul knew he needed to know God at a deeper level. He needed to share in the process that led to the manifestation of that power. What that means to us today is that there is an often overlooked but direct correlation between knowing God in the full-ness of His sufferings and experiencing the power of God.

Far too many people want a long-distance relationship with God—and only on the good days at that. When it comes to suffer-ing, we are part of a culture that seeks to avoid it at all costs. But then, we also want to have the resurrection power that comes from God. Yet, without increased intimacy, there can be very little—or even no—supernatural intrusions in life. No breakthroughs. No come-backs. No witnessing heaven being brought to bear on earth. None of that comes apart from intimacy with God. This is because His resurrection power is tied to knowing Him in spirit and truth. It's not tied to knowing Him from afar; it's tied to knowing Him closely.

And last I checked, there can't be a resurrection without some suffering first. A resurrection only takes place once something is dead. When Paul wrote of "being conformed to His death," he will-ingly surrendered his rights, goals, and life to God. He literally lived out Romans 12:1, which says, "I urge you, brethren, by the mercies of God, to present your bodies a living and holy sacrifice, acceptable to God, which is your spiritual service of worship."

A "sacrifice" in biblical times was dead. The priest did not place a live animal on the altar, letting it roam around and then taking it down—all the while calling that a "sacrifice." Being a "living and holy sacrifice" is essentially releasing your claim to your will, direc-tion, and purpose while surrendering all to God and His rightful claim on your life.

Paul's participation in the fellowship of Christ's sufferings increased his intimacy with Him as well. Suffering often does that.

Have you ever gone through a traumatic situation with someone only to discover, on the other side of it, you feel a closeness with the other person that wasn't there before? Whether the experience is something as minimal as two-a-day football practices in the summer or something more difficult, such as a health trauma, house fire, or natural act of God, suffering has a way of drawing people closer together.

I'll never forget the power of collective suffering and how an experience in Texas was manifested before the entire country as ravaging floods hit the Houston area some years ago. While our nation had been in the hot seat of racial divide and discord in the weeks leading up to the floods, it was in this time of mutual struggle that people of all races sacrificed their own well-being for the good of others. Multitudes of boat owners flocked to the region to search for and rescue those in need. Neighbors joined arms to bring help any way they could. Those who could not go to Houston sent money to supply those who could. And what had been a time of great divide in our nation in previous months melted into a time of shared grief and support.

Suffering has a way of bringing the best out of people. It also opens up eyes and hearts to a greater level of compassion, understanding, and appreciation than is experienced in seasons of plenty. When we seek to fellowship with Jesus in His sufferings, we are seeking to know Him at a heart level like none other. In visiting His pain through our own, we discover His character and attributes for ourselves. It's more than just reading about them in the Bible. It's coming to know and believe that He is trustworthy, empathetic, authentic, kind, consistent. and caring—even when life is at its worst.

Suffering is an invitation to closeness.

That's why James said, "Consider it all joy, my brethren, when you encounter various trials" (1:2). In the trial, your character is being conformed to the image and likeness of the character of Jesus Christ. Like the process of burning off impurities while refining gold, the end result is a purity that exceeds most anything else in value. That's why when you are facing difficulties and challenges in your life, it is good to ask God what it is He is seeking to accomplish both in and through you. Ask Him for wisdom in order to participate in the process of purifying your spirit to reflect His.

During times of trial, we normally look for a way to get out of the experience. Rather than seek the purpose in the pain, we search for the exit. But God has an intended outcome for what He allows in your life, and He will let the trial remain or allow another similar trial to occur as He shapes you into the character that brings you the most good and Him the most glory. See, knowing God isn't about reciting Bible verses or clocking in at church. Knowing God involves a spirit linking at such a level that you trust His sovereignty even when you don't understand it.

Have you ever experienced pain at the hands of a doctor or surgeon? Maybe you had to have a root canal. Regardless of the procedure, it was your trust in the doctor that gave you the calm you needed to endure it. You knew that his intention was not to hurt you but to make you better.

When God allows suffering in our lives, His intention is not to deliberately hurt us just for spite. Rather, God crafts our character and prepares us for our purpose through the shaping of our souls in suffering. Remember, Jesus didn't experience Easter Sunday until He first went through a bad Friday. He had to suffer before the resurrection.

Now, don't get me wrong. I'm not saying you should go out and look for opportunities to suffer. What I am saying is that when you do encounter suffering, you can recognize it as an invitation to draw near to God. Why? Because there is nothing like knowing God when He brings you through something as only He can do. That's when you get to know Him at a whole other level. And that's when you discover the things in you that you need to let go of, the parts that need to die. Becoming like Christ means releasing your sinful propensities and proclivities while embracing His holiness and grace.

Do you want to know God on a deep and intimate level? Then you need to participate in His process of ridding you of that which is contrary to Him. As He draws you nearer to Him in order to fellowship with Him, there will inevitably be sins He will want to remove in order to conform you to His likeness.

Have you ever taken a poker and put it inside the fireplace? When you do, the tip of the poker begins to turn red. The heat of the fire rubs off on the poker. But the fire is only able to rub off on the poker when the poker is in proximity to the fire. As long as the poker is sitting outside the fireplace, it will never gain heat. But once you start allowing it to abide in the midst of the fire itself, it will begin to absorb the heat of its environment.

The reason why so many of us as believers are not on fire for Jesus Christ is that we are not hanging out with Him, where He is. Rather, we remain outside His location and hang out in places we think will be considered "close enough" without being too close so as to feel the heat. But remaining what most consider to be a safe distance away means never knowing what it truly means to be lit up for the Lord. Never knowing what it means to experience for yourself the power of His resurrection, to witness His deliverance, favor, and grace in full force.

Are you lit up in your relationship with God? Are you lit up as you go out into the world, carrying the flame of His Spirit? Do other people see your passion, fire, and zeal for God and want to know how they can have the same? Or are you content to be a run-of-the-mill believer, understanding that God has power but never fully discovering how to access it, while situations and relationships in your life remain lost, dead, or unable to be resurrected?

Friend, life includes loss. Life will have pain. Life comes with suffering. But how you view and respond to that suffering will make all the difference in the world. If you choose to nurse your wounds, complain about your issues, and live in a spirit of regret and resentment, the pain will produce nothing but more of the same. God invites each of us into a truly transformative process in which He asks us to view life's trials through the lens of His own personal fellowship, intimacy, and purpose. When you choose to see life that way, you will also experience His power to restore, revive, and return the years that the locusts have stolen (Joel 2:25).

6

KNOWING GOD
IN YOUR SPIRIT

As we have been discovering together, the way to know that you know God is through change. If you are not changing, you're not growing in your knowledge of God. Knowing God experientially produces change. The transformation is the demonstration that the information has taken root. Thus, if you are the same as you always have been, not moving more toward the character and conduct of God (in your attitudes, actions, perceptions, and decisions), it is because you are not growing in your knowing of Him.

But what are you to do if you are accumulating information without experiencing transformation? If you are going to church, reading Scripture, and spending time in His presence but feel like you're just going through a process? I would like to suggest that you might be seeking to know God in your soul but not yet in your spirit.

In a well-known passage, Paul makes this statement: "To us God revealed them through the Spirit; for the Spirit searches all things, even the depths of God" (1 Corinthians 2:10). In this verse, God tells us that the way He reveals or discloses Himself to us is through the Spirit. When there is no spiritual connection, there is likewise no disclosure.

I'm sure you know people in your life at various levels. Some of those people you know only barely, others more casually, and then there are some you probably think you know fairly well. Yet even of those people you think you know fairly well, there is so much you don't know at all.

Have you ever read or listened to a news report about a person who wound up doing something heinous or egregious, and when the reporter interviewed those who knew him or her, comments surfaced like, "I didn't know they were capable of that," or, "That doesn't seem like them"? How much we know of other people—and, if we are honest, even how much we know of our true selves—is limited. How many times have you done or said something, only to think later, "That's not me"? You shocked yourself with your own propensity or response to something.

This being so, our inability to figure out God ought not to surprise us. If we can't figure out other people, let alone ourselves, it should not shock us that understanding God on the human level is impossible. He is the great un-figure-out-able God. Which is why coming to know God on any level at all requires His revelation and disclosure of who He is to us. No one can know God apart from Him giving them the ability, capacity, and opportunity to do so.

ON GOD'S TERMS

Paul writes in Romans 11:33, "Oh, the depth of the riches both of the wisdom and knowledge of God! How unsearchable are His judgments and unfathomable His ways!" He is simply *unfathomable*. You can't Google God and get any real results. The search engines won't locate Him for you. As theologians often say in reference to God, "He is wholly other." What that means is that He sits outside the realm of the finite because He is infinite.

The term *revelation* refers to those moments in our lives where God unveils Himself. He pulls back the curtain and allows us to see Him. Similar to how He passed by Moses in the cleft of the rock, allowing Moses to see Him while also protecting how much he saw, God has given us a way to know and understand Him as much as we are able through the presence and power of the Holy Spirit.

To come to know God, you must come to know Him on a spirit level, which is counterintuitive to how we typically function. We are made up of three parts: body, soul, and spirit. Our body interacts with the physical world through our five senses, which enable us to engage life in the tangible realm. Our soul is the self-life. It is our personhood, which includes our intellect, emotions, and will. And the spirit is the deepest part of us, which has been created to operate in the spiritual realm. It is also the part of us which is able to have contact with God.

Because so much of our lives involve our emotions and the concrete world in which we live, we have come to depend on these aspects of our makeup to guide us through life. Yet when God exposes Himself to us and draws us close for a deep connection with Him, it happens at the spirit level. And it blows our minds. Paul explains,

> We speak God's wisdom in a mystery, the hidden wisdom which God predestined before the ages to our glory; the wisdom which none of the rulers of this age has understood...but just as it is written, "Things which eye has not seen and ear has not heard, and which have not entered the heart of man, all that God has prepared for those who love Him" (1 Corinthians 2:7-9).

This Scripture is not referring to heaven in the sweet by-and-by. No, it is talking about earth in the nasty here and now. It is talking about what can happen in our lives when we come to know God more intimately. When God is interfacing with you on the spirit level, it will involve things that your eyes have never seen. It will involve things that your ears have never heard. It will involve things that your mind could never come up with on its own. Like I said, it will blow your mind.

God is beyond our five senses. His ways are beyond our capacity or ability to conjure up. And yet, we have blocked the knowing of God, or at least limited it, by either our bodies or our souls. As our five senses engage with the world around us, we expect that is how we are to engage with God. So we look for Him in ways we can see, touch, or comprehend. All the while we shut off the connection within our spirit that He longs to make.

Knowing God goes deeper than your physical ability. The experiential knowledge of God involves more than your personhood or senses. It resonates only in the depths of your spirit. Similar to how a deep-sea diver must put on special swimwear and carry an oxygen tank in order to penetrate the depths of the ocean, knowing God sits outside our normal abilities to discern. It is a journey of discovery that in and of itself requires discovery of how to go about the experience.

Far too many believers are stuck, though, skimming the surface like a Jet Ski on the ocean waves rather than risking the unknown of who God truly is. In order to go deeper with God, we must do so through the provision of the Holy Spirit. He enables "deep-God diving" beneath our natural, physical frame of reference—beneath both the distortion and confusion of our souls.

It is the Holy Spirit who not only knows God fully, but who also knows us beyond what we can know or express about ourselves. We read about this in the following two passages.

> Who among men knows the thoughts of a man except the spirit of the man which is in him? Even so the thoughts of God no one knows except the Spirit of God (1 Corinthians 2:11).

> The Spirit also helps our weakness; for we do not know how to pray as we should, but the Spirit Himself intercedes for us with groanings too deep for words; and

He who searches the hearts knows what the mind of the Spirit is, because He intercedes for the saints according to the will of God (Romans 8:26-27).

Not only does the Spirit know and understand God as the third member of the Trinity, but He also relates to us in our human experience at a level greater than we know ourselves. Connecting our spirit with God's Spirit is what we often refer to as an "anointing." It involves receiving spiritual contact and information, which then enables us to experience God deeply. And each believer has that anointing.

This may surprise you, as it is common in our culture to refer to certain people as having the anointing, as if only certain people have it. Perhaps we think of a special musician, artist, or speaker. Yet John tells us that all believers in Christ have the anointing: "You have an anointing from the Holy One, and you all know" (1 John 2:20). Every Christian has the anointing.

You may be thinking, *But Tony, my anointing doesn't seem to be working.* And I can understand how you might draw that conclusion. But that doesn't mean you don't have it.

The way I can best explain this is to compare the anointing to something we are all familiar with—a satellite TV provider. Let's say your satellite TV provider puts a dish on top of your roof that enables you to connect with the satellite in outer space so that you can get a picture on the television in your den. The dish is the capacity you possess to receive the picture from a place you can neither go to nor see yourself.

But in order for that satellite TV provider to give you what you need, it needs to receive a signal and then translate it to your TV. Your TV gets the "revelation" from what has been positioned on your roof, drawing down images and sounds from the invisible realm.

Now, if you try to see a picture on your TV without turning on your receiver, it is not that you do not have a connection. Rather, it's that you have not engaged the connection in the manner it needs to be engaged in order to supply you with the images and sounds.

Similarly, when you became saved, you received the Holy Spirit implanted within you. That's the anointing. But if your spirit is not working or tuned in to God, who sends information through the Holy Spirit, you will not get a clear picture. You experience distortion and noise when you seek to know God through any other method than through His Spirit's revelation to you.

Knowing God must be done on His terms and in His way. Moses wouldn't have experienced God on the mountain if he had refused to hide in the cleft of the rock as God passed by. He may have experienced something, but it wouldn't have been the deep revelation of God Himself. It is only when we seek God on His terms and in His way that we will be equipped with the necessary components for knowing Him.

THE APPRAISAL PROCESS

Paul tells us that when we connect with the Spirit, we open up the pathway for God to freely give us all we need for understanding and growth. He writes in 1 Corinthians 2:12, "Now we have received, not the spirit of the world, but the Spirit who is from God, so that we may know the things freely given to us by God." In other words, God doesn't want you going to the world for help or wisdom. He doesn't want you going outside the spiritual realm in order to see or experience truth. God knows that the physical realm does not contain the equipment or receivers necessary to access something so deep. That's not the connection you need.

But the Holy Spirit freely supplies all that God has stored up for you. The knowledge of God is freely given, at no cost. Yet many believers and churchgoers look to the world for direction on how to live, how to be a church, or how to experience the fullness of life. They look to the world for the healing, power, or deliverance that only God can supply. What's more, they even find the world's wisdom resonates most with them, not God's wisdom. As 1 Corinthians 2:14 says, "A natural man does not accept the things of the Spirit of God, for they are foolishness to him; and he cannot understand them, because they are spiritually appraised."

A "natural man" is an unbeliever who cannot access their spiritual receiver, so they go about their life—making choices, speaking thoughts, and evaluating decisions—based on what the world says is right and valuable.

A carnal Christian is a believer who has a spiritual receiver that is not being utilized. "I, brethren, could not speak to you as to spiritual men, but as to men of flesh, as to infants in Christ" (1 Corinthians 3:1). Infants move through life completely dependent upon the direction of others around them. Infants also allow their emotions and physical needs to control and dictate their actions. When Paul compares carnal Christians to "infants in Christ," he is explaining how a lack of spiritual connection leads to a lack of spiritual maturity. A person cannot know God fully when a pursuit of self (their own wants, needs, and desires) is the driving force. Knowing God takes place when self is set aside, thus enabling the spirit to place one's thoughts, feelings, and actions in cadence with God's Spirit.

Once you become a Christian, the Holy Spirit invades your human spirit, and the two are merged in such a way that you can now freely receive the things given to you by God. One of the things God gives freely is wisdom and discernment (James 1:5). And one of the things you are to do with that wisdom and discernment is to analyze aspects of life. First Corinthians 2:15 says, "He who is spiritual appraises all things, yet he himself is appraised by no one."

When you appraise something, you analyze it to determine its value. The spiritually minded person uses an appraisal process to determine whether the thoughts they are considering are consistent with the Spirit's way of thinking. The spiritual person is not first and foremost concerned with what other people think or even with what their own emotions are urging them to do. The spiritual person has another appraisal process altogether, one based on discerning what the Holy Spirit says about a matter. And unless that question is situated at the forefront of your thoughts, you are not yet functioning from a completely spiritual mind-set.

Yes, you are a Christian if you have trusted Christ, but you may not be spiritually minded. And those who are not spiritually minded do not experience God to the fullest capacity.

Paul expands on this thought about appraisal when he writes, "Who has known the mind of the Lord, that he will instruct Him?

But we have the mind of Christ" (1 Corinthians 2:16). In light of what he said previously (in verse 15), he further emphasizes the point that a spiritual person appraises all things but is appraised by no one. The reason being that no one possesses the ability to tell God what to do. After all, God never had to go to school to be instructed by anyone. God didn't have to rack up degrees to hang on His wall. God doesn't Google, surfing the internet for answers to questions that plague His mind. He requires no instruction on the subjects of health, mental wellness, or physics. God knows what He knows simply because He knows what He knows.

See, everything that you and I know came through a process of learning or discovery. But for God, His knowledge and understanding are immediate, infinite, absolute, and comprehensive at all times and on all matters. He does not look to anyone to be instructed by them, and He certainly doesn't look to His followers for an appraisal of Him. Rather, His mind is perfect, and He has made it available to each of us through the mind of Christ.

When Jesus walked the earth, He was in constant communication with the Father. We read often of Jesus going off to a remote place to spend time talking with the Father. They were in sync. That high-level communication saved Jesus time. Why? Because He didn't have to learn anything through trial and error. He was in such perfect contact with the Father that He got everything right the first time. There was no wasted life or time.

As you discover more and more how to tap into the Holy Spirit residing within you and giving you the mind of Christ, you also can progressively keep from making wrong decisions or saying the wrong thing. When you access God's thinking on the front end of decisions and conversations, based on His Word, you operate from a vantage point of perfect understanding.

Our refusal to first evaluate our circumstances spiritually causes our dilemmas in life at various levels. As we continue to insist on living according to the world's wisdom and the knowledge found through our five senses, we remain locked in a cycle of perpetual defeat and fruitless pain and uncertainty. Living life with the mind of Christ means tapping into His wisdom supplied through the revelation of the Spirit as He illuminates the understanding and application of God's Word in our lives. No, the Bible does not speak to the details of every specific issue you may face, like which job to take or whom to marry or what car to buy, but God's Word does provide spiritual principles that the Holy Spirit then uses to guide you in making wise choices.

Consider a copy machine. It simply replicates on paper whatever you place in the machine. When you push the button to start the process, a light comes on, and the machine captures and transfers the image on the glass to a sheet of paper. You then wind up with a replica of what you put on the glass through a transfer of illumination.

God is urging you to know Him more fully by tapping into His illumination that He has sealed within you in order to create copies of His wisdom, thoughts, perspective, and desires in your own mind, will, and emotions. Thus, you become a copy of what the Holy Spirit illuminates to you from the mind of God, experiencing the transfer of His being into your life as the thoughts of Christ are merged with your own thoughts.

Do you want to know God in your spirit? He has made Himself available to be known by you right now.

7

GROWING YOUR
KNOWLEDGE
OF GOD

As you are well aware, five plus five gives you ten. Ten plus ten gives you twenty. But when you move from addition to multiplication, you increase your results so much faster. Five times five gives you twenty-five. Ten times ten produces one hundred. But how does this relate to knowing God? The apostle Peter introduces us to the concept of multiplying our efforts of growth in 2 Peter 2.

We know from 2 Peter 1:1 that Peter is writing to Christians: "Simon Peter, a bond-servant and apostle of Jesus Christ, to those who have received a faith of the same kind as ours, by the righteousness of our God and Savior, Jesus Christ." Understanding the audience to whom Peter is writing is critical in identifying the application of the principles he presents. I want to underscore the fact that what he says in this book is aimed at born-again believers. Thus, when he talks about growing in our knowledge of God, he is not sharing how to be saved, but rather how we are to grow in our experiential knowledge of God as believers.

In fact, Peter is so committed to the believers' growth in the knowledge of God that he mentions it time and again.

> Like newborn babies, long for the pure milk of the word, so that by it you may grow in respect to salvation (1 Peter 2:2).

> Grace and peace be multiplied to you in the knowledge of God and of Jesus our Lord (2 Peter 1:2).

> His divine power has granted to us everything pertaining to life and godliness, through the true knowledge of Him who called us by His own glory and excellence (2 Peter 1:3).

> If these qualities are yours and are increasing, they render you neither useless nor unfruitful in the true knowledge of our Lord Jesus Christ (2 Peter 1:8).

> Grow in the grace and knowledge of our Lord and Savior Jesus Christ (2 Peter 3:18).

We see that Peter is concerned that we enter into what he refers to as the *gnosis* of God (in 2 Peter 3:18). *Gnosis* is the Greek word we translate as *knowledge*. *Gnosis* signifies a full or true knowledge of something. Or, to put it another way, it means an authentic knowledge. Peter is not concerned with how many Bible verses people can quote or how many times they attend church. Neither is he concerned with how many references to God people make over the course of their lifetimes. He is concerned about believers having a *gnosis* experience of God Himself through the power and grace of "our God and Savior, Jesus Christ" (2 Peter 1:1). This knowledge is to determine the course of our lives (Titus 2:11-13).

GRACE, PEACE, AND DESTINY

Peter tells us that when this experience takes place, we benefit greatly.

> Grace and peace be multiplied to you in the knowledge of God and of Jesus our Lord; seeing that His divine power has granted to us everything pertaining to life and godliness, through the true knowledge of Him who called us by His own glory and excellence (2 Peter 1:2-3).

This brings us to the multiplication concept I referenced earlier. Peter informs us in this passage that both grace and peace are multiplied to us as a direct result of knowing God intimately through His Son, Jesus our Lord. Not only that, but it is in knowing God that we have access to everything we need pertaining to life itself. In other words, if you desire to have more grace or peace in your life, you need to pursue the knowledge of God. Or, conversely, when you lack knowledge of God, you also lack the experience of His grace and peace.

Grace is what God is free to do for us because of what Jesus Christ has done. Grace is the inexhaustible goodness of God that cannot be earned, is not deserved, and can never be repaid. Grace is always free to you, but it is costly to God. It involves His unmerited favor. If you want to experience more favor, you have to have a deeper knowledge of God.

Peace is the ability to be calm no matter what chaos is going on around you. If you want more calm in the midst of life's storms, you must expand your experiential knowledge of God. There is a cause-and-effect relationship between knowledge of God and the quality of your emotional and tangible life.

Peter encourages his readers, saying that there is a way to do more than add a little bit of grace or peace to their lives. He speaks of multiplying the effects of both in all that we do.

In 2 Corinthians 9:8, we discover more about this power of grace and its impact on our ability to accomplish all we were created to do: "God is able to make all grace abound to you, so that always having all sufficiency in everything, you may have an abundance for every good deed." With grace comes the abundance and provision we need to carry out life's mission. But when we lack God's grace and favor in our lives, we also lack what we need to live out our destiny.

Far too many people today live as if they are entitled to their destiny. They name it, claim it, and then become disappointed when it doesn't show up on their doorstep. Yet biblical example after example illustrates the direct tie between the deep knowing of God (including the fellowship of His sufferings) and deliverance into a destiny. When you see someone who has risen to some level of influential prominence in the spiritual sphere on earth, you can pretty much be assured that there were seasons of sacrifice which drove this person to know God authentically.

It is in the knowing of God that you will find the pathway to your purpose.

Peter explains, "His divine power has granted to us everything pertaining to life and godliness, through the true knowledge of Him who called us by His own glory and excellence" (2 Peter 1:3).

You already have everything you need to meet all of life's demands in a way that will please God. The problem arises when you don't know you have it. If you don't realize that you already have it, then you don't know where to go get it. And if you don't know where to go get it, you will wind up looking in places that can't offer it. At best, the world offers a cheap substitute.

When new life is created within a woman, the DNA of that new life is contained within the fertilized egg. Everything that baby will grow to have—eye color, skin color, arms, legs—all that information is planted within the DNA. The conception process supplies to the embryo everything that life will need from then on.

A baby doesn't have to search for toddlerhood. A toddler doesn't have to go on a quest to become a teenager. And a teenager certainly doesn't have to hunt for adulthood. Each stage of life is inherent within the DNA of the life itself. What stops us from knowing all the idiosyncrasies of the new life from the beginning is the course of development.

Similarly, God tells us that there is a seed planted within us that contains the "DNA" prescribing all we need to live as He intended. All that you are looking for "pertaining to life and godliness" resides within you through the seed of the divine nature. Whether you desire joy, peace, wisdom, spiritual power, or self-control, it is through the development of the divine nature inside you that you will come to access these at a greater level. Development comes as you grow in your knowledge of God.

Keep in mind, the rate of your development is largely dependent upon your participation in it. For example, if a toddler refused to eat, the toddler's development would be stunted. If an adolescent refused to sleep, the adolescent's development would be stunted. In the same way, God has given you all you need to grow and develop spiritually, but the rate of that growth depends on your participation in the process. Peter tells us, "You have been born again not of seed which is perishable but imperishable, that is, through the living and enduring word of God" (1 Peter 1:23).

The DNA of deity lives within you in seed form. When God's Spirit entered your spirit, you received a new nature. It isn't fully grown in you and will not grow properly unless you participate in its growth. The reason more and more people are failing to experience the benefits of the DNA of God in everyday life is that they have not invested in the nurture and care of the divine nature. Thus, it remains dormant, like a seed in winter, unable to develop and express itself through life. It is the growth of the seed that produces the experience of God. When the seed remains dormant, the sin-damaged soul continues to dominate.

THE DISTORTED SOUL

When you came to Christ for the forgiveness of your sins, God saved you for heaven completely. But He saves you on earth progressively. It is possible to be delivered for heaven and be undelivered on earth.

This is because our souls are defective at birth due to inherited sin. They continue to be defective as we grow based on our experiences, the information we take in, and the pain and positives of life. Every soul is distorted. Like when a television is unable to get reception, the picture of our soul is fuzzy.

The problem is that we often settle for what I call "soul management." We try to make our souls better through commitments, seminars, New Year's resolutions, attending church, and serving in ministries. We mean well, but the soul cannot fix itself.

Our souls have been damaged by sin, some worse than others. Maybe you can manage your soul better than your neighbor, spouse, friend, or coworker can manage theirs. Maybe you have better self-control or discipline. But maybe you haven't had the negative experiences that they have, so it's not really a fair comparison.

Maybe you don't have an abusive or absent father. Maybe you haven't experienced racial discrimination. Maybe you've never gone hungry. Maybe you've never had perfectionist expectations put on you. The extent of our distortion varies, but we are all dealing with a distorted soul because the bacteria of sin has been distributed throughout our lives as we've grown.

The soul needs to be fixed. It needs to be brought to the cross. It needs to be transformed. This is hard to accomplish because the soul is so critically tied to who you are. Your soul is *you*. It comprises not only your mind, but also your emotions and will.

You are not your body. Your body is simply a container for your soul. Your soul is your essence.

When a person dies, their soul will either go to heaven or hell. The problem with our souls is that they have been contaminated since birth, making them distorted. Have you ever been to an amusement park and seen the mirrors that make you look fat, skinny, tall, short, or crooked? This is what has happened to our souls. To varying degrees, the effects of sin have engrafted themselves into our souls. Our souls need to be fixed, but they can't fix themselves.

Most of the time we try to get the soul to fix the soul, but that works just about as well as getting something distorted to fix the distortion. God doesn't want us to focus on managing the distortion. Distortion will always be distortion, no matter how well it is managed. What God offers is soul transformation.

Sure, we might be able to manage certain parts of our souls for certain lengths of time and to certain degrees, but our souls can never deliver themselves, make themselves better, or set themselves free. Only Jesus can do that. Jesus died on the cross not just to take your soul to heaven, but also to deliver your soul on earth (James 1:21).

But before deliverance can occur, a death must occur. Jesus said that if we want to be His disciples, we must "take up [our] cross daily" and follow Him (Luke 9:23). The cross symbolizes an instrument of death.

In order for your soul to become fully alive, it must first die to self. And it will need to die daily. Every morning when you wake up, don't think about how you can manage your soul. Instead, think about what part of your soul is not in alignment with God and ask Him to let that part die. As long as you try to keep your soul alive, it will continue to be distorted. You will never experience the freedom in life that you were meant to experience through your Creator until your soul dies.

What needs to die is your self-life, your viewpoint on a matter, your selfish thoughts. Not only does your soul need to die, but a new life needs to grow within it. This new life first comes to you as the "seed" we saw earlier in 1 Peter 1:23. This is your new nature.

But there are many Christians who have this seed and are still wondering why the Christian life doesn't seem to be working for them. They try their hand at soul management but end up being frustrated because the results are only temporary. The reason why the seed of the new nature is not working to bring about transformation for them is because the seed has not been allowed to expand in the soul.

The expansion of the seed affects the control of the soul.

Did you know that popcorn pops due to an explosion of moisture? Every kernel of popcorn has moisture in it. When you put popcorn in the microwave, the microwave heats up the moisture, creating steam. When steam rises inside the shell of the popcorn, it presses against the shell until the shell can't withstand the pressure anymore and pops open.

What once was a small, hard object has now increased in size and become soft and fluffy. In fact, when the popcorn pops, it's hard to even find evidence of the shell. The old outward appearance is now dominated by the inside characteristics.

Deep down in your soul, God has seated something that is ready to respond to the right environment. When the Holy Spirit begins to "cook" your divine nature so that the steam of your new life rises and presses through this outer shell called the body, you begin to "pop." You start to look, act, talk, and walk differently because of the change occurring on the inside. But until that change happens, the self-life will continue to rule even though you have the spirit life within you. As long as the spirit life is still in "kernel" form and has not been allowed to expand, it will remain unchanged. Any time you have a seed that is not given the environment to expand, it will not express life. It *has* life, but it won't express it.

GROWING THE SEED

Your body will only behave differently when the Spirit begins to dictate to your soul, not the other way around. One of the ways to grow the seed of the divine nature within you is given by Peter. He says,

> By these He has granted to us His precious and mag-
> nificent promises, so that by them you may become
> partakers of the divine nature, having escaped the
> corruption that is in the world by lust. Now for this
> very reason also, applying all diligence, in your faith
> supply moral excellence, and in your moral excel-
> lence, knowledge, and in your knowledge, self-control,
> and in your self-control, perseverance, and in your

perseverance, godliness, and in your godliness, brotherly kindness, and in your brotherly kindness, love
(2 Peter 1:4-7).

How do you grow the seed within you? It is a process that requires
diligence. It is not something you can casually pursue. To grow the
divine nature within you, you will need to apply yourself fully to
the supplying of seven key elements. Just as seeds of corn need soil
and water to grow into stalks of corn, the seed of the divine nature
within you needs seven things for it to be able to grow in a way that
influences your soul. This doesn't mean you are adding to what God
has already done in you, since the new nature is complete (Colossians 2:10), but it does mean that you are facilitating the growth and
expansion of the seed in your soul by feeding it healthy ingredients.

1. Moral Excellence

The first of the seven things you are to supply is moral excellence.
Another term for this is *virtue*. Supplying moral excellence simply
means giving something what it needs in order to fulfill what it was
designed to do. For example, if you sharpen a knife, you have now
given the knife virtue or excellence. In sharpening the knife, you
have increased its capacity to do what it was designed to do. A knife
that is dull lacks excellence as far as cutting is concerned. But when
it is finely sharpened, the knife has virtue.

We need to supply ourselves with what we need to live out what
we were designed to do. Peter tells us what this is in 2 Peter 3:18,
which says, "Grow in the grace and knowledge of our Lord and

Savior Jesus Christ. To Him be the glory, both now and to the day of eternity." You were made to bring glory to God. That's the DNA of your divine design. Thus, if you want the seed in your spirit to expand, you must add to it the goal of glorifying God. As 1 Corinthians 10:31 says, "Whether, then, you eat or drink or whatever you do, do all to the glory of God." You must live with the consciousness of glorifying God in order to live with the virtue He has designed you to have.

How does that play out in everyday life? You begin to ask yourself questions such as, "How will this action make God look?" or, "How will this choice expand how God is viewed by those around me?" or, "What can I do to bring glory to God and please Him?" When you become functionally conscious of the purpose of your spiritual growth, which is to bring God glory, you have added moral excellence to your faith. As you continue to seek the spreading of His glory, the seed of His divine nature will continue to expand within you.

2. Knowledge

Secondly, we are instructed to add knowledge to our moral excellence. To put it another way, you cannot grow beyond what you know. Once you see how God wants you to glorify Him, you are to look for additional ways to do more of that. What God is telling us through this passage is that we are to expand our faith in Him by adding knowledge to our understanding of how to glorify Him.

Start exploring ways that you can bring Him glory. Look for patterns in how He operates and how others respond to what you do or say regarding Him. If you discover an area where you can bring God glory, then study how you can increase that even more. The seed expands within you when you seek to make God's will your own through pursuing that which brings Him pleasure and advertises who He is.

3. Self-Control

Thirdly, we are instructed to add self-control to our knowledge and moral excellence. Self-control means disciplining yourself in a manner that enables you to maximize your skills at a higher level. It is a term often used with regard to athletes. Self-control comes through focusing on what matters most while allowing the distractions of life to fall by the wayside.

The enemy likes nothing more than taking you off the track of glorifying God. He does that through various ways—ways that may not even seem like temptations. He goads you into giving up your self-control. Whether you choose to indulge in too much entertainment, too many self-centered interests, or even plain laziness, a lack of self-control is one of the major detriments to spiritual growth.

Can you imagine how successful a professional athlete would be if they did not have the self-control to hit the gym in the early morning hours during the season? I can tell you right now, that athlete wouldn't be successful at all. When it comes to working out, few of us enter the gym simply because we want to do so. Rather, it is self-control that tells the body that even though sleeping in under the warm covers would be nice, the only way to prepare for the upcoming game is by getting up and working out.

Self-control is about so much more than just avoiding something. It is the discipline that is required in order to pursue what is good, right, and spiritually productive.

4. Perseverance

Fourthly, Peter tells us that we are to add perseverance to our self-control, knowledge, and moral excellence in order to nurture and develop the spiritual seed within us. Perseverance, in common language, means to hang in there and not throw in the towel. When the term is used in Scripture, it often refers to those seasons when you are experiencing a rough time. The reason why God doesn't want you to throw in the towel is because He knows that persevering develops your spiritual muscles of faith, hope, and trust. The harder life becomes, the closer you can move toward Christ. Hang on to God even when you don't see anything happening in your favor, because persevering positions you for a life of spiritual longevity.

5. Godliness

After perseverance, Peter says to add godliness. Godliness involves aligning your thoughts, words, and actions under the comprehensive rule of God over every area of your life. Godliness is not about how many times you go to church. Rather, it is about surrendering your will to God's will. It involves a spirit of humility and gratitude, because godliness acknowledges the reality that all good comes from above (James 1:17). There is no room for pride in godliness. Godliness is a quiet, gentle awareness of God's rule and authority over all.

6. Brotherly Kindness

To godliness, we are instructed to add brotherly kindness. The Greek term used for this is *philadelphia*, referring to a love that is rooted in friendship, respect, affection, and selflessness. It means an extension of love to another member in the body of Christ, pouring your life into them through the grace of God flowing from you. When you choose to extend brotherly kindness to someone else, the Lord often uses that as a boomerang to bring kindness back to you (Luke 6:38).

Thus, if you are battling depression, as tough as it may be, seek to minister to someone else who may be depressed. If you are going through marital struggles, seek to minister to another couple who is also struggling. If you need healing, help someone else who is sick as well. If you need financial victory, give to someone else in a spirit of love. Brotherly kindness is the demonstration of the love you've already received from God Himself. It is the outward manifestation of the fruit of that love.

7. Love

It is in extending brotherly kindness that the next element— love—shines through, even to unbelievers. And the authentic application of all seven of these qualities causes you to bear fruit in your knowledge of God. Second Peter 1:8 says, "If you possess these qualities in increasing measure, they will keep you from being ineffective and unproductive in your knowledge of our Lord Jesus Christ" (NIV).

Knowing God involves so much more than reading books about Him or singing songs of praise. While these things are important, they are not the end in themselves. Rather, the qualities of virtue, knowledge, self-control, perseverance, godliness, kindness, and love are the demonstration that the information about God has taken root within you.

God has a lot of children who claim to know Him but display little or no fruit. They are still Christians—saved by grace—but little is coming from their lives to bring God glory and advance His kingdom.

Fruit has three distinct qualities to it, and spiritual fruit is no different. First, fruit is always visible. Second, fruit always bears the character of the tree from which it came. Apple trees don't bear pears or oranges; they grow apples. Third, fruit is always for the benefit of someone else. Any fruit that is eating itself is known as rotten fruit. Fruit exists to nourish and delight someone else.

If you ever want to gauge how well you know God, all you need to do is look to the fruit of your life. Does your spirit reflect the qualities we just read about in 2 Peter? Is the fruit God is producing through you benefiting others, or are you looking to gain from it yourself?

Peter has harsh words for those believers who fail to bear character-based fruit. He writes, "Whoever does not have them is nearsighted and blind, forgetting that they have been cleansed from their past sins" (2 Peter 1:9 NIV). Peter calls these Christians "blind." This is because an awareness of our sins and what God has truly saved us from produces hearts that mirror His own. It is only when we allow pride to deceive us, causing us to forget the manifold mercies of God—like Lucifer, who sought to overtake the throne of

God (Isaiah 14:12-15 KJV)—that our hearts become hardened to love, kindness, and godliness.

Whenever we forget the cross, whenever we marginalize Calvary, we are in trouble. Knowing God fully and freely begins at the foot of the cross, where the forgiveness of our sins tore the veil which once separated us from Him (Matthew 27:51). That, and only that, is our foundation for knowing Him.

When you do know God from that vantage point, you will become fruitful. Life will become meaningful. Your spirit will overflow to those around you in such an impactful way that they cannot help but notice that there is something different about you. Something that draws them, like you, to God—to know Him more deeply than ever before. That, my friend, is what you were made for.

Part 2

THE PRIVILEGES

8

EXPERIENCING DELIVERANCE

You can know when God plans to show you something new about Himself.

You can know when God is wanting you to draw closer to Him and know Him at a deeper level.

You can know when God desires to manifest His glory to you in ways yet unseen.

You can know when He wants to become more real to you at a level you've never experienced before.

How can you know all these things? You know this when you are in a crisis.

See, a crisis is not just a crisis. It's never just a crisis. It is an opportunity to experience and know God to a degree and depth that you have never known before.

Did you sigh as you read that last paragraph? If I were there with you, perhaps you would turn to me and say, "Okay, Tony, that's nice, but I really don't want to know God that well after all. I'm satisfied right where I am. I don't want a crisis."

I understand. After all, who wants to go through a crisis? No one dreams of their next crisis. No one hopes for a crisis around the corner. No one longs for a crisis. Rather, the reverse holds true. Most of us look for a way out of a crisis even if we simply see one on the horizon. We run from crisis. And yet a crisis provides a prime opportunity for us to experience and know God intimately, personally, and profoundly.

When God wanted to reveal Himself at another level to someone in Scripture, it nearly always followed the consistent pattern of crisis. He either allowed or created a crisis. During these times, people would find themselves in situations which they themselves could not fix. They came upon predicaments they could not unravel on their own. They ran into circumstances they could not circumvent. They were in a crisis.

You know you are in a crisis when all your options are gone. When everything you thought could work doesn't work. You can't negotiate your way out of it. You can't spend your way out of it. You can't talk your way out of it. You can't network your way out of it. When all you have learned and tried is not enough to alleviate the situation, you know you are in a God-ordained or God-allowed crisis with a purpose.

MORE THAN YOU CAN BEAR

There is a myth in Christianity that I often hear people repeat: "God will not put more on me than I can bear." Maybe you've heard this. Maybe you've said it. Some people even think it's in the Bible. But let me debunk that myth right now with a look at the life of Paul.

In 2 Corinthians, Paul wrote, "We do not want you to be unaware, brethren, of our affliction…that we were burdened excessively, beyond our strength, so that we despaired even of life" (1:8).

If ever there was a hopeless situation, Paul was in it. Paul hadn't done anything to cause it. In fact, he had followed God's leading straight into a place of despair.

If you feel desperate today, you are in good company. The apostle Paul was a man who served God, knew God, and pursued God's calling at all costs. That right there should demonstrate to us that a life of service to our King doesn't guarantee a life without difficulties, sorrow, or sacrifice. In fact, the opposite is typically true.

God sometimes allows situations in your life to appear hopeless because He is trying to direct your focus onto Him. You may feel like giving up because you can't seem to fix the situation, and no one you know can fix it either. All your human resources have been depleted. But Paul reveals a key principle in his next statement: "Indeed, we had the sentence of death within ourselves so that we would not trust in ourselves, but in God who raises the dead…He on whom we have set our hope" (2 Corinthians 1:9-10).

In order to take Paul deeper in faith, God put him in a situation that his abilities and connections could not change. Why? So that Paul would learn to trust God even more so than he had thus far.

Is God being mean in these situations? No.

I understand it may feel that way when you're going through a difficult time, but what He's really doing is trying to take you deeper. Because it is in these times—these hopeless scenarios where you see no way up, over, or out, and yet God ultimately "raises the dead" for you—that God becomes experientially real to you.

Seek Him when life's situations have you struggling (Isaiah 55:6). Don't be ashamed of the pain or despair you feel. Paul himself felt it. Never deny your emotions. Simply turn them Godward and look to the one who knows how to raise the dead.

If you're not dying or in a situation that is dying—relational, financial, emotional, or otherwise—you will never know what it is to experience a resurrection. If you don't need one, you won't see one.

It's one thing to say that God is a healer when you are not sick. It's a whole different ball game when you are sick. Knowing He is a way maker when you are not lost is a different kind of "knowing" from those times when you are lost. It's one thing to say that God is a provider when your refrigerator is full. It's a whole other type of claim when your refrigerator is empty.

God allows crisis situations in our lives because, in them, we discover Him in a way we have never known Him before. When He wants to move us to a new level of intimacy with Him, He will typically use a crisis. For example, when the Israelites fled Egypt on their way to the promised land, God allowed them to run into a dead end. He allowed them to get pushed up against the Red Sea. But in allowing them to reach the end of themselves, He also allowed them to witness what He could do when there were no more options on the table.

You probably know some non- or nominal Christian friends who don't think much about God while they are doing okay. They don't need Him when their bank account is full, they are healthy, and all seems to be going well. This may even describe you and me at times. When we get comfortable, it's easy to rely on our own wisdom, strength, and thoughts rather than depend heavily on God. When we get comfortable, we can get stuck.

This is what happened to the Israelites when they were slaves in Egypt. Their work wasn't too hard at one point. They had good food to eat. And yet, God wanted them to move on from there and enter the promised land. The problem was that the Israelites were comfortable in their bondage. So God allowed a crisis. He allowed things to get worse in order that they could one day get much better.

We read about this in Exodus 1:

> Now a new king arose over Egypt, who did not know Joseph. He said to his people, "Behold, the people of the sons of Israel are more and mightier than we. Come, let us deal wisely with them, or else they will multiply and in the event of war, they will also join themselves to those who hate us, and fight against us and depart from the land." So they appointed taskmasters over them to afflict them with hard labor. And they built for Pharaoh storage cities, Pithom and Raamses. But the more they afflicted them, the more they multiplied and the more they spread out, so that they were in dread of the sons of Israel. The Egyptians compelled

the sons of Israel to labor rigorously; and they made
their lives bitter with hard labor in mortar and bricks
and at all kinds of labor in the field, all their labors
which they rigorously imposed on them (verses 8-14).

The situation kept getting worse for the Israelites in order for
God to draw them nearer to Him and nearer to His plan. Eventually,
they cried out to God.

Now it came about in the course of those many days
that the king of Egypt died. And the sons of Israel
sighed because of the bondage, and they cried out;
and their cry for help because of their bondage rose
up to God. So God heard their groaning (2:23-24).

It was in the midst of an ongoing crisis that the Israelites learned
to seek the Lord. They cried out so much that it says their cry literally
"rose up to God." It went as high as the heavens. This wasn't
a polite prayer. This was an ugly-cry prayer. But when your life is
breaking apart, the ugly-cry prayers are all you've got. You don't
have the strength for sophisticated, high-sounding, studious, and
theologically accurate prayers. You are like Peter sinking beneath
the waves, yelling at the top of his lungs for Christ to save him right
then and there (Matthew 14:30).

The purpose of trials and crises in your life is often to get you to
cry out to God and then see Him come to your deliverance. When
this happens, you get to know His power, presence, and purpose at
a higher level than ever before. You come to know God in ways you
could never know Him when life is simply comfortable.

THE LONG PATH

While most of us assume all blessings include favor and pleasant circumstances, God shows us that He can also bless us through pain. A downturn in your situation can actually be a blessing which puts you on an upward path.

It was the Israelites' added stress as slaves in Egypt that caused them to cry out to God, which then caused Him to respond to their cry, ushering in their eventual freedom and the establishment of their own nation. Scripture tells us that God will often shake things up in order to usher in something new (see Hebrews 12:25-28).

Never look at your crisis as merely a negative situation you must endure. Many crises are positives disguised as pain. They are God reaching into your life and placing you on a pathway to your purpose.

Exodus 2:25 tells us that when the Israelites cried out to God, "God saw the sons of Israel, and God took notice of them." To take notice of someone is to pay special attention to them. When you are in a crisis, you want special attention. You don't want general information from God. No, when you are up against the wall, you want God to get very specific in your scenario. Which is exactly what God did for the Israelites. In fact, as they cried out to Him, God worked on their solution.

When Scripture was written, it did not include chapters and verses like what we read today. Each book was penned as one ongoing piece of literature. So, when we read about the Israelites crying out to God in the last part of Exodus 2, and then we see God's response in the first part of Exodus 3, we know the reality is that these two things happened back to back.

The Israelites cried out to God for deliverance.

And God showed up to a man named Moses, who was shepherding his father-in-law's flock of sheep.

God didn't just show up, though. He showed up in a *burning bush*. Connect the dots. They don't seem connectable, but God doesn't operate according to human wisdom. In other words, God rarely makes sense to us, but He does make miracles.

This burning bush was not consumed by the fire; rather, it hosted God's presence as He gave Moses his calling. Since Moses knew that when bushes burned in the dry desert, they burned up into nothing, and yet this one did not—a seeming contradiction of nature— he chose to move closer and take a look.

As Moses came closer, God told him to take off his shoes because the ground he walked on was "holy ground" (Exodus 3:5). Then God gave him his calling to go deliver the Israelites from the oppression of the Egyptians. He raised up Moses as the answer to the people's prayer. The Israelites probably wouldn't have guessed that answer would be an older shepherd on the back side of the wilderness.

But that's the problem we run into when we face our own crisis situations as well. We look for answers we can understand. We look for solutions we can take part in. But the truth of the matter is that God may have your solution somewhere far removed. What's more, your solution may be facing its own dilemmas and contradictions as well. It could be in its own burning-bush scenario. But once your solution aligns under God's command, then God can create a divine intersection between the solution and the crisis. He will bring together all that is needed to connect your crisis with His provision.

You know the story. Moses proceeded to approach Pharaoh on behalf of God to issue freedom for the Israelites. Pharaoh resisted until ten plagues sent by God convinced him otherwise. The Israelites were released—and yet, even after they had been released, Pharaoh changed his mind and chased after them.

Had God led the Israelites along the shortest route to the promised land, they never would have come upon the Red Sea and been trapped. But Scripture tells us that God led them on the longer route. The reason is that they would have faced the Philistines on the shorter route and run straight into a war they were not prepared to fight (Exodus 13:17-18). They would have been slaughtered. Thus, God took them toward a body of water they could not cross, one He would part for them.

Friend, if it seems like God is taking the long path in leading you to victory or freedom, keep in mind that He always has a reason. The enemies and battles on the shorter path may be too much for you. He may be leading you in the direction of His intervention. He may be wanting to demonstrate His faithfulness to you, because as you learn lessons on His faithfulness, you will gain the confidence, faith, and insight needed to wage those larger wars down the road.

Scripture tells us that God Himself hardened Pharaoh's heart (i.e., intensified his rebellion) so that he would chase after the Israelites (Exodus 14:4). In other words, God was setting up a schooling situation for His children. He wanted them to experience a crisis so that they could also learn how to depend on Him. This lesson would be critical later on, when He would bring them into a promised land inhabited by skilled warriors. God had just delivered the Israelites from one crisis in Egypt, but He needed to have them experience Him at a whole new level through this next crisis. So He made the Egyptians chase after them.

This was no small chase either. Exodus 14:6-7 tells us that the Egyptians set out with more than 600 chariots. The sounds of the horses and chariots would have been enough to frighten even the stoutest of men. But keep in mind, the Israelites were a community of elderly people, women, and children as well. I imagine their hearts beat as fast and as loud as the hooves. As a result, the people once again cried out to God. They complained to Moses and told him that it would have been better for them to have died in Egypt than to face a slaughter by the Red Sea (verses 10-12).

Moses' response was simple and straightforward.

> Moses said to the people, "Do not fear! Stand by and see the salvation of the LORD which He will accomplish for you today; for the Egyptians whom you have seen today, you will never see them again forever. The LORD will fight for you while you keep silent" (verses 13-14).

In today's language, these verses might read, "Shut up! Shut up! Shut up! And watch what God will do!"

As Moses looked to God, God provided the solution. God told Moses to lift up his staff, stretch it out over the waters in order to divide the waters, and direct the Israelites to cross over on dry land (verse 16). Sounds well and good. But that's because we know the rest of the story. How do you think Moses felt when he heard those instructions? Might he have questioned his own sanity? He had just led these people out of bondage and into a certain-death situation, and the solution was to hold his puny little shepherd's staff over a body of water that would surely swallow them all up?

I wonder if his voice shook or his hand trembled as he obeyed God's command. I wonder if he lifted his rod high or just barely enough to count as obedience. Before the waters actually divided, I'm sure Moses looked like a fool. But faith will often make you feel like a fool, because God wants to see if you trust Him or if you trust yourself more.

To experience spiritual deliverance in your life, though, you must exercise faith. You must. There is no way around this. You must hold out your rod over whatever sea God is asking you to face. When He sees your faith, He responds—just like He did with Moses. When Moses lifted the rod, the waters divided, and the Israelites crossed over on dry land.

Did you catch that? They crossed over on dry land. They didn't get bogged down in the muddy bottom of the sea. Their carts and horses didn't get stuck. God not only divided the sea for them, but He also dried up the land so that they could cross over. This was two miracles in one.

What's more, the Egyptians would never have chased after them had they not also been able to move across the dry land. But God needed them to chase after the Israelites so that when the Egyptians made it to the middle of the sea, He could close the waters over them, destroying them instantly. What was the result? Exactly what God had wanted.

> When Israel saw the great power which the LORD
> had used against the Egyptians, the people feared the
> LORD, and they believed in the LORD and in His ser-
> vant Moses (Exodus 14:31).

The Israelites saw God's power. They feared God, and they believed in Him and Moses. They came to know God and His delivering power for themselves.

Which is exactly what He wants for you too. And He will let you get to the bottom of whatever situation you are in to teach you just that. He will let you get down to your last dollar. He'll let you think you might lose your home. He'll let you suffer issues at work that seem out of control. He will allow circumstances that don't look like they are in your favor. But instead of grumbling and complaining, look to God. Recognize the opportunity in front of you for God to show Himself strong. He can deliver you, tweak the troubles, turn the situation around—flip, twist, and override whatever Egyptians are staring you down.

I know it may look like you are facing your own Red Sea. I realize it may seem like the devil has you hemmed in or your boss is in control. I understand that the economy may appear to be dictating your life or your relationships have become strained beyond what you can fix. But if you will tighten your grip around whatever God has placed in your hand and, with boldness, lift it in faith over the sea that looms in front of you, you will come to know God for yourself in a new and personal way as you experience His deliverance on your behalf.

Your crisis will not have the last word. God, and God alone, has the final say. Trust Him, even when life doesn't seem to make sense, knowing that His presence is powerful enough to turn everything around—suddenly. And when He does, your faith will grow, God will get greater glory (Exodus 14:4,17), and the knowledge of Him will spread (Joshua 2:9-11).

9

EXPERIENCING POWER

There's a story about an older woman who lived way out in the boondocks, far away from access to running water and electricity. Eventually, a philanthropist took it upon himself to run cables out to her area, providing her with electricity. However, after a few months, the power company noticed that she barely used any power at all.

Seeking to be of service, the company sent someone to her home to inquire as to why she wasn't getting the power they had run out to her. The representative knocked on her door, and when she appeared he asked, "Ma'am, are you using the electricity that we've run to your property?"

"Oh yes, I am," she replied promptly with a toothless grin.

The representative scratched his head and continued, "Well, our records indicate that you are barely using any at all. Do you mind telling me how you go about using it?"

"It's very simple," she said. "When it begins to get dark, I turn on the lights y'all gave me just long enough to light my kerosene lamps. Then I turn them off."

I'm sure you'll agree with me that this lady didn't quite understand the use of the power that had been given to her. She had the power, but she wasn't maximizing it. She wasn't getting out of it all that the electricity had been designed to deliver.

While this illustration may seem ludicrous, many of us do something similar on an even larger scale. After all, we sing songs and tell others about God's power. We are not unaware of the deposits God has made in us, yet so many believers today are entirely powerless.

Why is this so? It is due in large part to the disconnect we have between knowing God and experiencing His power. Like the woman in the boondocks, we've come to rely on what we know—our own efforts—and only get a taste of what God has gone to great lengths to provide for us. Somehow, it makes us feel safer to remain in our comfort zone, no matter how limiting that comfort zone actually is.

Yet when you know God as He wants to be known—when you experience Him as He wants to be experienced—the result is a spiritual power that enables you to overcome, resist, and discern. It is a spiritual power designed to equip you with all you need for life and godliness (2 Peter 1:3). It can strengthen, restore, guide, and inspire you. Without it, you are left to meander through life by the dim light of a candle. With it, you have all you need to fully live out the abundant life Christ died to procure for you.

DON'T LOSE HEART

The apostle Paul introduces us to this power in Ephesians 3:13, where he makes this statement: "I ask you not to lose heart." To "lose heart" means to become discouraged or despondent, to quit, to give up or throw in the towel. It's an "I can't take it anymore" mentality. And there is a lot in this day and age to lose heart over. It might be a financial situation or a relationship. It could be a health concern, career issue, or emotional distress. Whatever the cause, losing heart occurs when your get-up-and-go has gotten up and gone.

Maybe you had to force yourself to pick up this book. Maybe this thought has crossed your mind: *Why am I reading yet another Christian book when so little has changed up to this point?* You're tired, weary, and worn out. For you, losing heart means that hope is nowhere to be found.

Paul understood that mind-set. He'd been there himself. At one point, he even despaired of life (2 Corinthians 1:8). In today's terminology, we'd call that suicidal. Paul knew a thing or two about "losing heart."

I've known my share of despair, as I'm sure you have too. But that's why it's so critical to understand how to access a power greater than our own. When our power is not adequate, we must tap into the power which is supplied to us through abiding in God Himself.

Paul shares with us the first thing we are to do when we struggle with losing heart. In Ephesians 3:14, he tells us what he did: "For this reason I bow my knees before the Father." Due to the propensity in and around him toward losing heart, he did what he knew to do—he dropped to his knees.

When somebody drops down to their knees, it means they are in a serious, humbled kind of prayer. They are going low under the Father in heaven. Paul crouched, as Elijah did when he fervently prayed for rain (1 Kings 18:42). Once he did, Paul went on to pray a very revealing prayer about power. He asked on behalf of those who were losing heart in Ephesus, "that [God] would grant you, according to the riches of His glory, to be strengthened with power through His Spirit in the inner man" (Ephesians 3:16).

Paul asked for the kind of power that would occur in the inner man. This power, brought about through the Holy Spirit, is a power that enables believers to no longer allow their circumstances to own them. It's a power to deal with a losing-heart situation.

Have you ever been in a situation where you needed this kind of power? Maybe you are in one now. Maybe you don't feel like you have the power to get out of the scenario, reverse the circumstances, deal with life's pain and loneliness, or even ascertain the direction you should go.

Paul addresses this context, saying that the answer to the problem that is causing you to lose heart does not sit outside of you. It does not involve changing the situation itself. It does not include altering the circumstances, erasing life's pain, or coming up with your own method of overcoming.

Paul is saying that the power to overcome what you may feel you are succumbing to is based on the Spirit's work inside you. This kind of power is only accessed through intimately knowing God and tapping into the life He's placed within you.

I realize this is likely the opposite of your inclination. When we're losing heart about a situation, we typically take steps to escape whatever it is that is causing the pain. And while that's a very natural thing to do—creating distractions, masking the pain, or participating in activities to numb it—such a solution is only temporary. Once the distraction disappears or the numbing wears off, the tendency to lose heart remains. And the reality that life somehow manages to go on with its daily demands only seems to compound the despair.

In those times, merely coping may be the dream. But Paul has told us the secret to doing more than that! The secret rests in a great power inside you that you may never have suspected was there. But like a battery needing to be charged in order to supply the power for a device to function, you as a believer in Christ need to know how to access this inner strength of God's Spirit to give you what you need to make it through life's difficulties.

Paul informs us that in those moments, days, weeks, and years when we are running around frantically, desperately seeking to stem the tide of "losing heart" that rises within us, we will gain the power we need in the inner man alone. He gives us insight into how this works in Ephesians 3:17-19, saying, "That Christ may dwell in your hearts through faith; and that you, being rooted and grounded in love, may be able to comprehend with all the saints what is the breadth and length and height and depth, and to know the love of

Christ which surpasses knowledge, that you may be filled up to all the fullness of God."

The word *dwell* in verse 17 means to make oneself at home. It means to abide, loiter, hang out, and relax in the presence of someone. Consider how most of us have a welcome sign on our front door or a mat that proclaims the same sentiment to any visitors who stop by our house. Oftentimes, when we invite visitors in, we add the phrase, "Make yourself at home." Yet this phrase is one of our greatest lies in American culture, because it's not what we mean to say at all. If we were to be honest with our guests, we'd say, "Make yourself at 'room.'" Or, at best, "Make yourself at 'two rooms'—this one, and the powder room down the hall."

When we welcome someone into our home, we are not inviting them into our bedroom, closets, and study areas. We're being polite, but we aren't being honest. Because if guests made themselves at home, they'd probably wind up seeing the junk we threw into the back rooms in order to make the front room look neat and livable when they arrived.

Yet when Paul instructs us to let Christ dwell in our hearts, he wants us to allow Jesus to make Himself at home—in the true sense of the phrase. Far too often we treat Jesus like we do the guests at our door. He's allowed to come into the rooms we have tidied up and straightened, but not into those places we'd rather He not see. We let Jesus into those areas of our hearts that we feel He'll be pleased with, all the while slamming the door shut when we don't want Him to notice or influence how we keep a room. But in order for Jesus to dwell in our hearts in such a way that we experience

His full power, we must invite and allow Him to dwell fully, freely, and entirely.

Jesus must be free to go into the dirty garage, where you have stuff stacked end on end. He must be free to go to the library of your mind and witness all that you allow into your thoughts. He must be free to visit the living room, where your fellowship with friends takes place. He must be free to visit your bedroom and even peer underneath your bed and in your closet to see what you've stashed away.

When Paul says that Jesus is to dwell in our hearts, he means Jesus must be free to roam everywhere.

One of the reasons we seek to keep Jesus from roaming freely in our hearts is because we are ashamed of what He might come across. But you are only hurting and limiting yourself by living in that mind-set. Jesus already knows everything about you. Your refusal to open up to Him in prayer or to allow His presence to have full reign only reduces the strength you receive from Him to overcome that which brings you shame.

There is nothing you can hide from Jesus. He already knows all. The reason why it is so critical to give Him full access into the most vulnerable places of your heart is so that you can have more power. Limited access for Christ results in limited power from Christ, which leads to more despondency, more discouragement, more failure, and more shame.

Jesus must be free to make Himself at home even in the messiest areas of your heart. When He does, you will "be able to comprehend with all the saints what is the breadth and length and height and depth, and to know the love of Christ which surpasses knowledge, that you may be filled up to all the fullness of God" (Ephesians 3:18-19). Knowing God includes authentically inviting God to know *you*. Only when you allow Him access to yourself will He fill you completely with His strength in your inner self. It is in dwelling with Christ and Him dwelling with you that you get to know the love of Christ that "surpasses knowledge," experiencing the reality of God operating in your life without bounds or limitations.

I know you may be losing heart. I understand you may be tired. Perhaps you are discouraged. But the only way to turn those negative emotions around is to discover the love of God that comes through knowing Him intimately. As Jesus dwells in you, you become "rooted and grounded" in His relationship with you (verse 17). See, God is not just after academics; He's after intimacy. And until God is able to expand His presence in you because He's free to roam in all areas of your heart, you will not deepen your intimacy with Him.

Intimacy is always based on trust, awareness, and honesty. It is intimacy which releases the Spirit's power in your life. The Holy Spirit is not merely a nice addendum to the Christian faith; He is at the heart and core of it. He is not merely a force or influence; He is the third person of the Trinity. The ministry of the Holy Spirit has been promised to us by God. If everything in life emanates from the knowledge of God, then it's safe to say that everything in the spiritual life emanates from the knowledge of the Holy Spirit.

A RESERVOIR OF POWER

All it takes is several hours or even mere minutes without

electricity to make us realize how much we benefit from it. Electricity is power. Stick a piece of metal in one of your outlets, and you will become one of the lights in your home. Electricity is also exceedingly powerful in providing ways to cool and cook our food, freeze water, and make bread pop out of a toaster. When it's dark, the lights come on, because we have an "invisible" power available to us.

The power of electricity is very real and readily available, whether or not we choose to use it. And if we mess with it in the wrong way, electricity can also discipline us.

But the power we have in our homes is nothing compared to the power that all of us who know Jesus Christ have in our lives in the person of the Holy Spirit. He is the invisible presence and power of God.

The Spirit is deposited into the life of every believer at the moment of salvation, and He will never abandon us. He is a royal resident in our lives. One of the Spirit's most important roles is to empower us to live supernaturally. He is also the invisible power source for the collective body of believers, the church. Acts 1 gives us a classic passage that addresses this topic. The centerpiece of this text is a very familiar verse:

> You will receive power when the Holy Spirit has come upon you; and you shall be My witnesses both in Jerusalem, and in all Judea and Samaria, and even to the remotest part of the earth (verse 8).

The clear implication of Jesus' words is that the disciples would not have power until the Spirit came. Spiritual power is not simply a concept to be understood but a reality to be experienced. If you have the Holy Spirit living within you, you have as much of Jesus as those first disciples had, even though Jesus lived among them for more than three years. You do not have to go back in time to be with Jesus. He is with you right now in the person of the Holy Spirit. That is why the Holy Spirit is sometimes called the "Spirit of Christ" (e.g., Romans 8:9; Philippians 1:19).

You have as much spiritual potential as any other believer, because you have the Spirit in all His fullness. He can take you into a realm that you in your natural state could never enter: the realm of spiritual power. It is the Spirit's power that Paul references in Ephesians 3:20. We read, "Now to Him who is able to do far more abundantly beyond all that we ask or think, according to the power that works within us."

This is a spiritual power that exceeds anything we could ever imagine. This verse is not talking about the routine aspects of life. This verse is talking about the things you cannot come up with on your own. It's when God comes through for you in ways you don't expect. When He comes from left field, and you're looking right. When He blows your mind, and all you can do is sit back and say, "Wow!"

This is the power the Spirit supplies when we dwell with Christ, and Christ is in us completely. This is the power that comes in ways that no one can explain—when God opens doors that mankind has shut, overturns decisions that seem locked in place, and enables you to get through something you never thought you could survive. When God comes through in a way that is unpredictable—a way you could not manufacture on your own—this is the power Paul says is yours for the taking, simply by abiding in God and knowing Him (and being known by Him) deeply.

While Ephesians 3:20 is a verse that believers in churches all across the world love to quote, post, and claim, there is a condition in this passage that we often overlook. In fact, when someone proclaims this passage, they usually speak loudly at the start and then whisper the last part. This is because the beginning talks of what we want so badly: for God to do far more than we ask or imagine. But the end of the verse tells us how this happens. It is done "according to the power that works within us."

God looks at the power within before He determines the action without. If there is no abiding power within because Jesus Christ is not at home in your heart, then you are not going to be filled to the fullness of the Spirit's power. You can't piggyback on someone else's testimony or faith to experience personal power for yourself. It is only in authentic intimacy with God Himself that you access the spiritual power you need.

When I was growing up in Baltimore, I would get together with my friends and swim every Saturday night when the fire marshal would come and open up the hydrant. That was our neighborhood "swimming pool." We'd all put on shorts, run outside, and play in the water gushing from the hydrant.

As I played in the water, my inquisitive mind became increasingly confused. While my eyes could see the three-foot pipe extending out of the ground that delivered the water to us, I could not understand how that much water could come from that small of a pipe. In fact, the water would gush for hours. And I'd wonder the whole time how it could be.

One day I asked my dad how that small hydrant could hold so much water. That's when he explained to me that the pipe in and of itself did not contain the water. The water, rather, came from the Druid Hill Reservoir. My father told me that the fire hydrant was just a delivery piece, making the water available to us.

My dad went on to explain that the water never ran out because even though massive amounts were released every Saturday, when the reservoir got low, rain would fill it back up. And as long as the hydrant was connected to the reservoir through a series of underground pipes, there would always be an abundance of water, whether it was being used for play or to save lives.

God is the reservoir of your power. You are simply the fire hydrant through which He wants to deliver life, happiness, and— most importantly—power. But there has to be a connection underneath in order for that power to come to you in times of play or need.

The problem is that we often focus on opening the tap rather than making certain the connection is secure. Without the connection in place, it doesn't matter if the hydrant is open or not. No power will come to us or through us without the abiding, connective presence of the Spirit of God through Jesus Christ.

Let me illustrate this another way. If you were to bring a thimble to the Pacific Ocean and fill it up, you would get a thimble's worth of the Pacific—but that's all you would get. Because once the water hits the top of the thimble, everything else spills back into the ocean simply because the thimble can't handle any more.

If you were to bring a glass to the Pacific Ocean and fill it up, you would certainly get more than a thimble's worth of the ocean. Yet you wouldn't get any more than a glassful, because once the water hits the top of the glass, it spills right back into where it came from.

If you were to bring a bucket, you would get more than a thimbleful and more than a glassful, but you wouldn't get more than a bucket's worth of the ocean, because that would be the entirety of your capacity. If you were to bring a barrel, you would get no more than a barrel's worth. And even if you were to bring a tanker, you would not get any more than a tanker's worth of ocean. When the tanker is full, you cannot hold any more water.

It's not that the Pacific Ocean runs out of water to give. No, the Pacific has as much water as you could ever need. But the ocean won't waste its water by trying to give you more than you have the capacity to hold.

A lot of us want a tanker's worth of blessings and spiritual power from God when we only have a thimbleful of relationship and intimacy with Him. We try to pray down blessings and power from heaven, all the while standing there with a small thimble or cup in our hands.

Let me remind you that *Jesus* is not a magic word to be used at your discretion. Jesus is Immanuel—"God with us"—who came so that you might know God and experience life abundantly through your abiding intimacy with Him, made manifest in the Spirit's power.

The amount of spiritual power in your life is tied directly to the size of the relational container you bring to God. It is "according to the power that works within [you]" that you realize the abundance of His provision for you.

When you are filled with the "fullness of God" (Ephesians 3:19), you are able to rise to the level for which God has created you. It's similar to an unfilled balloon and its inability to float in the air. Even if you were to toss an unfilled balloon as high as you could, it would still come right back down. But when you fill it with helium, the balloon takes flight. It is able to do more than an unfilled balloon ever could because it is now filled with the power it needs to rise and remain high.

I have power strips in my home. Power strips are useful when there are not enough outlets in certain locations. They give you more outlet potential. Once you plug in the power strip, you have multiple outlets where you once had only two. It enables you to power a number of things that you couldn't have powered without it. It's not that the electricity didn't exist, it's simply that you didn't have the capacity to handle additional power until the power strip was plugged in.

When God saved you, He did the internal wiring to supply you with all you need to live out the victorious Christian life. He placed the new nature inside you through the person of the Holy Spirit and, in so doing, laid the circuitry in place to supply you abundantly with His power. What God wants to see, though, is the kind of capacity you bring to Him.

Why should you pursue the knowledge of God? Not so you can pass someone's test, quote some verses, or gain academic information. Pursue knowing God so that you can access the power He's provided to you. Let God blow your mind with all that He has in store for you. The power is available to you. How willing are you to reach inward and get it?

10

EXPERIENCING
WISDOM

If you've ever traveled on State Route 1 in California, you know that it is treacherous driving. On one side sits the enormous expanse of the Pacific Ocean, with drops as frightening and dangerous as any could be. As you turn and twist around various bends and curves, you are faced with the sight of these drops.

On the other side tower hills and mountains so steep and looming that frequent signs announce their potential doom: "Watch for falling rocks." I'm not quite sure what a person could do in a car if they saw a falling rock, especially since the only other option involves a steep drop down to the ocean. But the signs are there nonetheless.

And then, as if that is not enough, the road becomes so narrow at many points that you wonder how two cars going in opposite directions are supposed to both get around the bend. What's more, the bends and curves appear so quickly that it is difficult to see if there are any oncoming cars to avoid.

I remember traveling along this road while on a family vacation years back. As I made my way up and down and all around this road, I heard voices from the backseats, saying, "Daddy, Daddy—please get off this road!" To appease the kids, I drove slower. But that still didn't take away all the fear.

Life itself is much like State Route 1. It's treacherous going. You never know what's around the bend. Sometimes if you look to the right, you see disaster. But if you look to the left, you see another form of disaster. And then, on top of that, the road becomes dangerously narrow at times. Oncoming issues approach you, often seemingly out of nowhere, barely giving you enough time to react in order to avoid them at all.

When a person drives on State Route 1, they must navigate carefully because there is impending danger mile after mile after mile. Similarly, life must be navigated carefully because there are so many twists and turns that bring risk and danger. You probably know what it is like to make a wrong turn on a narrow road in life. These wrong turns produce emotions of regret and shame. You realize that if you wouldn't have turned that way, you wouldn't be facing the mess of consequences that plague you today. If you wouldn't have made this decision, then life would have been different. Maybe life would have been better. So there looms a covering of sorrow when you don't carefully navigate the twists and turns of life.

But what does knowing God have to do with navigating life? The answer is simple: everything. The Bible has a word for navigating well—*wisdom*. This is God's word for understanding what decisions to make and which paths to avoid. Wisdom is God's provision for handling the twists, tweaks, turns, and precipices of life.

Most of us have cable television in our homes. When you have cable television, you have access to channels that cover just about any topic, entertainment choice, or interest in life. There are channels for sports, movies, cooking, health, exercise, shopping, and more. Hundreds of channels give cable subscribers the opportunity to become informed on a whole host of concepts and arenas in life. Yet, in all the plethora of channels, I have yet to come across a wisdom channel.

If there were ever a channel needed today, though, it's one on how to navigate life with all the decisions facing us on such enormous levels. Wisdom is designed to answer these questions:

> *How do I make choices carefully and correctly?*
> *How do I live in the best manner possible?*
> *How do I make the most of the gifts, time, and treasures God has given me?*
> *How do I position myself and my loved ones for emotional success?*

Wisdom answers these questions and more one by one. And gaining and accessing wisdom has everything to do with knowing

God. Paul says in Ephesians 1:17, "That the God of our Lord Jesus Christ, the Father of glory, may give to you a spirit of wisdom and of revelation in the knowledge of Him." In this verse, Paul directly correlates knowing God with having wisdom and revelation for life. Solomon also said that the knowledge of God is understanding (Proverbs 9:10).

To put it another way, to not know God is to not have wisdom. To not know God intimately is to miss out on knowing how to make the choices that are in your best interest.

Without a control tower to navigate the plane, the pilot flies blindly in a sea of traffic. Without a control tower, a pilot has no way of knowing how to avoid danger and, ultimately, the deaths of everyone on board. When there is no one who sits outside of the plane itself and is able to see more than the pilot can see, the pilot is open to all sorts of disasters. Yes, the crew and passengers may make it safely to their destination, but the chances are very slim.

When it comes to flying, especially flying in traffic, there must exist someone who can see beyond the pilot's view. Likewise, in life, knowing God provides revelation and wisdom that allow us to see beyond what we can see. Knowing God allows us to be aware of upcoming dangers so that we can avoid them. It allows us to be aware of better weather patterns so that we can climb to them, avoiding turbulence along the way. It allows us to navigate through life issues in such a way that not only gets us to our intended destination, but also gets us there happy, whole, and at peace.

You can't change yesterday. You can't erase last week. You can't undo last month, last year, or the last decade. But there is one thing you still have control over, and that is how you both act and react in the present. Because how you handle today has everything to do with what kind of tomorrow you experience and what rewards and pleasures you'll receive in eternity. It's wisdom that will get you where you need to go, maximizing your life choices and positioning you for greatness in the kingdom of God.

KNOWLEDGE AND UNDERSTANDING

Wisdom is effectively applying divine truth to everyday life situations. It's also known as the skill of "righteous living." It means you understand how to apply truth to your life choices through a God-given ability to perceive the absolute nature of a matter and implement the will of God regarding it.

Wisdom is completely Spirit-based decision making.

So important is this subject of wisdom that God dedicated a whole book to it: Proverbs. This book is often unread, and yet, in terms of making everyday choices, it is the most important book of the Bible. The whole theme of the book is wise decision making. In it, God speaks to us about finances, parenting, relationships, purity, our work, and much more. In Proverbs 2, the table is set for the entire book's focus on wisdom.

> My son, if you will receive my words and treasure my
> commandments within you, make your ear attentive
> to wisdom, incline your heart to understanding; for
> if you cry for discernment, lift your voice for under-
> standing; if you seek her as silver and search for her as
> for hidden treasures; then you will discern the fear of

the LORD and discover the knowledge of God. For the LORD gives wisdom; from His mouth come knowledge and understanding. He stores up sound wisdom for the upright; He is a shield to those who walk in integrity (verses 1-7).

This passage tells us about two specific things that are needed to live wisely: knowledge and understanding. When knowledge and understanding come together, they give birth to wisdom. If you are going to fully experience the benefit of wisdom that comes as a fruit of knowing God, you must first seek knowledge. Ignorance is not bliss when it comes to living life wisely. Many of us have made poor decisions simply because we did not have all the information.

By knowledge, I am referring to the ability to perceive the true nature of a matter. Have you ever jumped to a conclusion only to change your mind after obtaining more information that clarifies the information at hand? Having knowledge gives you the ability to go beyond the limitations of human understanding and tap into God-based understanding.

Like the person in the control tower helping the pilot fly safely, God's knowledge reaches beyond what we have the ability to discern on our own. He has access to the secret and hidden things that we could never know apart from Him giving us the ability to do so. Some people refer to this as *insight*. This is the Holy Spirit's transference of His viewpoint on a subject to us. As we saw in Proverbs 2:6, "The LORD gives wisdom." It cannot be purchased. It cannot be traded for. It cannot even be located apart from God. As we see in Job 28, it comes from our relationship with God Himself:

Where then does wisdom come from? And where is the place of understanding? Thus it is hidden from the eyes of all living and concealed from the birds of the sky. Abaddon and Death say, "With our ears we have heard a report of it."

God understands its way, and He knows its place. For He looks to the ends of the earth and sees everything under the heavens. When He imparted weight to the wind and meted out the waters by measure, when He set a limit for the rain and a course for the thunderbolt, then He saw it and declared it; He established it and also searched it out. And to man He said, "Behold, the fear of the Lord, that is wisdom; and to depart from evil is understanding" (verses 20-28).

Wisdom is located in God alone. To access that wisdom, you must fear God (Proverbs 1:7; 9:10). What does it mean to fear God? It means to reverence Him in the high esteem He deserves. It means to surrender to His kingdom rule over every area of your life—to seek His viewpoint based on His inerrant Word and to walk in its ways, rather than your own. To fear God involves a conscious awareness of His presence while allowing that awareness to impact your choices.

Wisdom is about so much more than just knowledge. It is a merging of understanding with that knowledge, which then plays into life application. Knowledge is perceiving the true nature of a matter. Understanding involves knowing what to do with that knowledge.

A story goes that a man had some machinery that had broken down. He didn't know how to repair it, so he called the repair technician. When the repairman came over to look at the machinery, he took out his toolbox, grabbed a tiny hammer, and hit the machine. All of a sudden, the machinery revved up.

The owner said, "Wow! How much is that going to cost?"

The repair technician then wrote him a bill for a thousand dollars.

"A thousand dollars?" the man asked in disbelief. "Break down the cost, because you barely did anything!"

The repair technician agreed to do so. As he scribbled onto the bill, he explained, "One dollar for the tap. Nine hundred ninety-nine dollars for knowing where to tap."

Understanding has to do with knowing "where to tap." While knowledge involves gathering the data and truth to inform your decisions, it is understanding that enables you to connect the proper purpose of that knowledge to the right choice.

It's amazing how people will spend billions of dollars on an industry that digs deep into the interior of our earth to pull out shiny minerals and gemstones, but most won't lift a finger to gain wisdom. Yet, just like diamonds and precious stones would lose their value if they were simply strewn all across the landscape to have at will, God doesn't set wisdom out in the open for each and every person to simply stumble upon it. As we saw in the Proverbs 2 passage, we are to look for wisdom as a person looks for silver and hidden treasures. This valuable commodity rests in the depths of God alone. His Spirit connects with our spirit to impart wisdom to us when we seek Him with all our heart, mind, and soul. In fact, in Ephesians 1:17, this gift is specifically called the "spirit of wisdom."

Wisdom is not an item on the shelf.

Wisdom is the Spirit.

In order to attain spiritual wisdom, you will need a close relationship with the Holy Spirit. This is found in knowing God fully. God longs for you to understand spiritual realities, but He knows the value of wisdom and won't divvy it out at random. It comes when you first understand and commit to a key principle in Scripture: "Seek first His kingdom and His righteousness, and all these things will be added to you" (Matthew 6:33). It is only in putting God first in your heart, thoughts, words, and actions as the ruler over all you do that you will gain access to what He holds for you—His wisdom.

HUMAN OR DIVINE?

The book of James offers us the most comprehensive contrast between human wisdom and divine wisdom.

> Who among you is wise and understanding? Let him show by his good behavior his deeds in the gentleness of wisdom. But if you have bitter jealousy and selfish ambition in your heart, do not be arrogant and so lie against the truth. This wisdom is not that which comes down from above, but is earthly, natural, demonic. For where jealousy and selfish ambition exist, there is disorder and every evil thing. But the wisdom from above is first pure, then peaceable, gentle, reasonable, full of mercy and good fruits, unwavering, without hypocrisy. And the seed whose fruit is righteousness is sown in peace by those who make peace (3:13-18).

James writes clearly that there are two ways of looking at things: man's point of view and God's point of view. Humanism comes in all shapes, sizes, and colors. As many people as you can talk to is as many opinions on what is right or wrong that you can get. Humanism changes based on who is doing the talking—and whose "truth" is being pronounced. God's point of view, on the other hand, remains steady throughout time. This is because His point of view is rooted and grounded in His unchangeable character and precepts.

Human wisdom and divine wisdom are mutually exclusive. They cannot operate in conjunction with each other. By virtue of their sources, they cancel each other out. And while human wisdom may provide you with temporary relief, divine wisdom provides you with the cure. Human wisdom majors on temporary solutions and is in league with the demonic, while God's wisdom operates from an eternal mind-set.

You might not know that I almost died as a teenager. I don't talk about this often, but when I was younger, I was a severe asthmatic. My asthma attacks were horrific. I'd be gasping for breath as my dad would rush me to the hospital. Once we would get to the hospital, the nurse or doctor would give me a shot to open up my lungs.

But on this one occasion, the intern gave me the wrong medicine. I'll never forget the look on my father's face as tears came to his eyes. Fear gripped him, as he wasn't sure if his son was going to make it. All of this happened due to an error by the clinician in giving me the wrong thing to try to make me better.

Thankfully, I survived this critical mistake, but it serves as a good illustration of what is happening to far too many people these days.

The world is serving up all kinds of wrong directions and solutions under the guise of "wisdom," leaving people gasping for air when they've already been struggling to breathe. Life is hard enough without getting fed false information to make it even worse.

But that's all human wisdom truly is. It's enough to whet your appetite for the moment and then leave you in a daze of confusion and disorder. That's why God calls human wisdom "foolish" (1 Corinthians 1:19-25).

When my son Jonathan was in college, he raised pit bulls. Jonathan has always had the entrepreneurial spirit, so he took it upon himself to raise and sell this breed. That was fine with us until he then took it upon himself to bring three of them home from college to our house one weekend. He had to secure them in the yard because we wouldn't let them in the house.

He tied them to a small lamppost we have in our backyard. But after a few hours, these three dogs had walked around the lamppost so many times that they were tangled up. Jonathan went outside to try to untie them, but the more he pulled the dogs backward to reverse them around the post, the more they would strain to go forward. This back-and-forth scenario went on for what seemed like an hour, and all the while the pit bulls gasped for air as they yanked even harder against Jonathan's direction.

If you've ever seen a pit bull, you know this is a breed with a big head. Yet with all that room to house a big brain, these dogs weren't smart enough to cooperate with Jonathan as he tried to unwrap them from the pole. No, they just wanted to go their own way—regardless of the pain it was causing them.

Too many of God's children have what we read about in James 3—a wisdom laced with selfish ambition and arrogance. They have a big head, thinking they know the right way to go. But instead of discovering the freedom they were saved to enjoy, they only find themselves chained tighter and tighter to life's circumstances, issues, and regrets. And while God, in His mercy, desires to deliver each of us from the chains of limited understanding, when we pull against Him, we only cause ourselves more pain.

Insisting on your own way will get you worse off than nowhere. It will get you stuck. And stuck is no way to live your life, my friend.

If you are stuck and feel like no matter what you do, life seems to keep going down the same path of problems, then it may be time to let go of human wisdom and surrender to God's wisdom through a deeper knowledge of Him. Living as a spiritual pit bull may make you feel like you are top dog, but in reality, it will get you nowhere at all.

Our sin and finiteness combine to distort the wisdom we gain on our own. That's what makes God different. He has no sin, and He is infinite. Thus, He can never make a bad calculation. He can never say, "Oops, I made a mistake." God knows all the information about any subject you raise to Him. The wisdom from above is the only true form of wisdom there is.

You can't mix human wisdom and godly wisdom and still arrive at the right decision. Just like you can't put half-unleaded, half-diesel gas in your car and expect it to run. If you do, the mixture will not only prevent you from getting anywhere, but it'll ruin your engine as well. That's why gas stations have different nozzles for those two different types of gas. The owners know how disastrous it would be if someone put the wrong gas in their car.

Similarly, seeking to live by both human wisdom and God's Spirit will effectively destroy the path you are on and turn you into a schizophrenic saint. God desires for you to be so filled with His Spirit that there is no room for humanity's way of erroneous thinking to even enter your mind. As you feed the spirit within you through an abiding relationship with the Lord, His presence and viewpoint begin to dominate your thoughts. When that happens, you don't have to search the internet for the answers you are seeking or call up ten carnal friends to give you advice on which way to go. When you are intimately close to God in such a way that your spirit moves in cadence with His own, you will grow in the wisdom you need for every choice you have to make. The Holy Spirit will share with your human spirit how to take the knowledge you have gained from God's perspective and apply it to whatever situation you are facing.

He does this in numerous ways. One way is by bringing thoughts to your mind that settle in your heart. These can come after you've gone to His Word to find out what He says about a certain principle or subject at hand. Yes, it may require some digging in Scripture and some time in meditation, but the Spirit will see you seeking wisdom as a person seeks silver, and He will provide what you need.

Wisdom is similar to a plane in that way—it takes you to a higher level of seeing. When you are in a plane, the world looks different down below compared to what you saw when you were down there. Distance gives you perspective, whether in a plane or in your spirit.

You are able to see the big picture and gain insight into the secret plans God has been trying to share with you all along. Most of the time, the things God leads you to do through the Holy Spirit will be different from what you would have come up with yourself. After all, who would think of defeating an enemy city by marching around the wall for six days, and on the seventh day marching around it seven times and then screaming? (See Joshua 6.)

If a military commander had initiated that plan, his army would have locked him up and thrown away the key. That's no strategy—that's insanity. But God knew it would work because He knows more about the physics of the world in which we live than the greatest scientists could ever know.

Who would think that God would take 30,000 men and tell Gideon to bring that number down to 300, because 30,000 was too many for the battle at hand? (See Judges 7.) Who ever heard of having *too many* soldiers?

And who would think that God would get Moses' attention through a bush that burned without burning up entirely? Or that He would provide salvation to all humanity through the virgin birth, substitutionary death, and victorious resurrection of the God-man? Or that He would tell the wisest man who had ever lived that the way he could find out the real mother of a baby was by saying that he was going to slice the baby in two? (See 1 Kings 3.)

These are not the normal ways of solving problems. God's ways are truly unsearchable (Romans 11:33-34).

But when God begins to share His thoughts with you because you are seeking Him first as if seeking silver itself, He will lead you as He led Joshua, Gideon, Moses, Solomon, and many others. When you commit your ways to the Lord, He will direct your path—because you are no longer leaning on your own understanding, but rather acknowledging Him so that He can guide you (Proverbs 3:5-6).

Yes, I understand that you cannot fix yesterday. Neither can I. And perhaps you are still reeling from some of the mistakes or bad decisions you have made. But let me tell you just how good God is at what He does. He can still hit a bull's-eye with a crooked stick or a broken bow. Even though you may be in a bad situation due to bad choices you've made, He can show you how to make the best of these scenarios. That's just how good and wise He is.

11

EXPERIENCING IDENTITY

There is a major crime afoot today that all of us need to be concerned about. We're warned about it on television virtually daily. We receive documents in the mail calling on us to protect ourselves from becoming a victim.

This crime is identity theft, when an unauthorized person takes your identity and uses it without your permission. The perpetrator uses your Social Security number, credit cards, or anything else that will benefit them.

I've experienced a form of this theft on numerous occasions in regard to social media. Impostors take the identity of a well-known preacher or ministry leader, duplicate that identity on a new page, load pictures they have swiped from the legitimate page, and then pretend to be that person. As they grow the page, they then reach out to followers, asking them to donate to causes like purchasing wells in Africa. But these donations do not go to the stated cause; rather, they go straight into the pockets of the people committing identity theft.

The ministry I govern would report these fraudulent pages every week to the various social media outlets, attempting to get them shut down. But inevitably more would pop back up. It became a vicious game of whack-a-mole. Some enterprising person eventually created software that follows a certain algorithm which enables these fraudulent accounts to be caught more thoroughly, and when we adopted this software, we shut down more than fifty fraudulent accounts in just one week!

Identity theft is no small thing. For a time I had people coming up to me and asking me if I were raising money for this cause or that, especially for wells in Africa. When I would tell them I wasn't, they would let me know about a fraudulent account asking them to send money. Thankfully, this became much less of a problem after we employed the use of the identity-theft software. But as you can see, great havoc is wrought when someone rips off another person's identity. Not only in my case with social media, but in other cases where various aspects of people's lives have been destroyed. They incur debt they didn't create. Their credit rating sinks due to no fault of their own. They face roadblocks on their path toward progress, which they had worked so hard to build. Identity theft ruins lives and topples dreams.

In the spiritual realm, identity theft takes place as well. The evil one wants to take from you what God has ordained for you. As Jesus said in John 10:10, the devil has one aim in mind when it comes to your life, and that is to destroy it. We read, "The thief comes only to steal and kill and destroy."

Bottom line: Satan wants to steal your life from you. He wants to ruin your life. Ruin your essence. Ruin who you are. This doesn't necessarily entail stealing your physical life through death. No, there are many ways in which Satan can ruin your life while you are still living. He can crush dreams. He seeks to scar souls. He ruins personal esteem, hope, relationships, finances, belief, and character. Satan can mess up your life so much that you don't even recognize who you are anymore.

But I have good news. One of the benefits of knowing God more fully and deeply is that when you discover who He is, you also discover who you truly are.

WHO ARE YOU?

People spend inordinate amounts of time and energy trying to discover themselves these days. Any approach to discovering ourselves that goes outside of God lies in the distorted reality we see through distorted lenses in a distorted, sin-infested world. Our identities have already been so messed up that we lack the ability to purely discern who we are, what we desire, and what defines us.

Some people were raised in situations and homes that messed up how they think about themselves and others. Some people have had such terrible experiences with other people that it has negatively affected how they perceive themselves and the world around them. The media also constantly inundates us with new definitions of what it means to be significant, valuable, female, male, beautiful, handsome, etc.

One enormous clue to the fact that millions of people have lost a primary connection point to their own personal and spiritual identity is the billions of dollars made every year from the sales of jerseys bearing some athlete's name on the back. Somehow, people feel that their own value rises when they attach someone else's identity to themselves through a name stitched on a shirt.

Now, you know your identity is off track when you spend your time wishing you were somebody else. Yet that's what happens every day on social media as people scroll through countless profiles, envying other people for their looks, what they have, or what they seemingly experience.

If you are spending your time wishing you were someone else, that means either you don't know who you are, or you don't think much of who you are because Satan has done a number on your identity in Jesus Christ.

You may have seen the series *Roots* on television many years ago. It was about a twentieth-century man going back in time to find out who he was by discovering from where he came. This quest consumed him. Why? Because identity is key. People are desperate for it. People pay for it. People compromise their integrity in an effort to establish it, find it, or change it. They get dressed up to establish it. Buy things to inform it. Exercise to create it. Get surgery to change it. But the problem is, like mannequins in department store windows, people can look as good as it gets but still not have life. They may simply be on stage looking good for a moment.

What happens when a person doesn't have life? The most common results run rampant in our culture today: depression, anxiety, worry, overspending, crash dieting, codependency, addiction. If you are defined by discouragement or a nagging sense of inner conflict, your spiritual identity has been swiped by Satan, and you are suffering the results of his heist.

Jesus came that you might "have life, and have it to the full" (John 10:10 NIV). He didn't just come to give you an ordinary existence. He made it clear that He came for you to experience the abundant life and all that it entails. In 2 Corinthians we read,

> He died for all, so that they who live might no longer live for themselves, but for Him who died and rose again on their behalf. Therefore from now on we recognize no one according to the flesh; even though we have known Christ according to the flesh, yet now we know Him in this way no longer (5:15-16).

Paul reminds us in this passage that we know no person according to the flesh. In other words, we are not to evaluate people merely by their physical appearance. The "flesh" refers to what we can see, hear, and touch. It refers to our human vantage point of determining who someone is. But Paul tells us that if we really want to understand the essence of a person, we can't do it through the grid of the flesh. If you view a person that way, you will be faked out.

We have all been faked out by someone in our past. He or she may have looked and sounded good, but they just didn't hold up to whom we thought they were portraying themselves to be when all was said and done. Which is why bringing God's viewpoint into everything is critical.

According to the Bible, our identity is not to be rooted in how we look, what we say, the job we have, or any other aspect of that nature. Our identity is first and foremost tied to our "new birth" in Jesus Christ. The apostle Paul makes it clear that knowing our identity in Christ helps us discover who we really are (Galatians 2:20). Those of us who have been saved by Jesus are a "new creation" (2 Corinthians 5:17 NIV). Just like a caterpillar is not a butterfly and a butterfly is not a caterpillar, we are not the same as our original flesh. We have become entirely new in our new birth in Jesus.

Knowing this and defining yourself by this is critical. Because if you define yourself wrongly, you'll function wrongly. If you define yourself rightly, then you will function rightly.

I once had a Chinese pastoral assistant who worked under me for a number of years while he went to seminary. Whenever he was required to provide his national origin on paperwork, he would always indicate he was Chinese. But due to his upbringing and surroundings, this man acted, spoke, and functioned as if he were black. What Paul is reminding us in this passage is that even though our origin is rooted in the flesh, our new creation is rooted in Jesus Christ. When we root our identity in Christ, we will have no confusion over how we are to act, speak, and function.

In our contemporary culture, we have far too many voices telling us who we are. We have too many whispers in our ears trying to define us. But only God ought to define us, because our identity comes from Him. If you are getting your self-definition from any other source but God, then it is flawed. When you choose to operate according to the flesh (i.e., your unredeemed humanity), that human perspective will always be flawed by sin, circumstances, history, and your background.

The reason why we are not discovering our true self-identity and, therefore, the purpose that we should derive from our identity is that we have allowed the flesh to identify us rather than the new creation.

Acts 17 is one of the most profound chapters in the Bible on God. It isn't a chapter that gets a lot of airtime, but it provides powerful truths related to our personal identities. Let's look at verses 24-28:

> The God who made the world and all things in it, since He is Lord of heaven and earth, does not dwell in temples made with hands; nor is He served by human hands, as though He needed anything, since He Himself gives to all people life and breath and all things; and He made from one man every nation of mankind to live on all the face of the earth, having determined their appointed times and the boundaries of their habitation, that they would seek God, if perhaps they might grope for Him and find Him, though He is not far from each one of us; for in Him we live and move and exist, as even some of your own poets have said, "For we also are His children."

It is in God that you "live and move and exist." It is in knowing Him that you come to know yourself. You are in Him, and He is in you. As you discover more fully who God is, you will also discover more fully who you are. But you will never truly come to know your own personal identity apart from God. Rather, you'll live your life in trial and error, simply trying to locate yourself. If you don't know whom you are looking for, how will you know when you have discovered yourself?

Far too many people waste an inordinate amount of time trying to discover who they are. They look to their job, their friends, or even their social status and accumulation of stuff. Yet, just as they seem to discover who they are, they find out it actually isn't who they are after all.

If you want to discover who you are, you will need to look to God, because you have been made in His image—and the new creation within you comes from Him. Sure, this new creation doesn't present itself easily. Just like when a caterpillar is transforming into a butterfly, there is always a transitional struggle. There's effort. It takes time. It's a battle for the butterfly to break free from the cocoon surrounding it.

Similarly, as your new nature inside you seeks to break free from the fleshly hold of the sin nature, it's going to require effort and intentionality on your part. This new creation in you wants to be free, but it is trapped and must struggle to break out. It is in the struggle that strength is developed. Just like a butterfly being released too soon from the cocoon and not having the strength to fly, the struggle of your new nature growing and becoming dominant within you gives it the ability to produce a completely transformed creation capable of carrying out God's purpose.

When you trusted Jesus Christ as your Savior, 2 Peter 1:4 says that you received within you the divine nature. God deposited His life in you in spirit form. The key to experiencing the fullness of this new nature comes in understanding what 1 Peter 1:23 says: "You have been born again not of seed which is perishable but imperishable, that is, through the living and enduring word of God." Thus, your new identity in Christ comes to you in seed form. As James 1:21 says, "Putting aside all filthiness and all that remains of wickedness, in humility receive the word implanted, which is able to save your souls."

Once you are saved, the new creation comes to abide within you as a seed. Yet, in order for the seed to realize its full potential, it must grow. For example, a watermelon seed is a very small seed that contains within it an enormous amount of potential for growth. Same with an acorn. Within that seed, which you can hold in the palm of your hand, rests the potential for an oak tree so large it could one day shade an entire house. But it will only do this if it is allowed to grow. If a watermelon seed or an acorn is not allowed to grow, no one will ever experience the potential contained within either of them.

Let that concept sink in. As believers in Jesus Christ, we have the divine nature placed within us—but it is placed within us as a seed. If that seed does not experience growth, then it also does not fully manifest all the benefits within its potential.

Why are so many believers not living with more victory, overcoming more strongholds, arising out of more difficulties than they are? Because they have not nurtured and cultivated the seed within them—the divine nature planted inside, which, unless it grows, does not supply life to the soul, leaving believers useless and fruitless in the Christian life (2 Peter 1:8-9).

Only when a seed is planted in the soil, which can give it life, will it grow. It doesn't matter if you pray for that seed, take that seed to church, or meditate about that seed. Unless the soil is there to provide the environment for growth, growth will not take place. It's all about the soil.

THE SEED PRINCIPLE

In Luke 8, Jesus told a story about a sower who goes out to sow seed, but the primary focus of this parable is on the types of soil in which the seed is cast. Jesus described four different types of environments for the seed: on the roadside, on rocky soil, among thorns, and on good soil (verses 5-8). In each case, the soil represents a particular kind of life and illustrates how that life responds to the seed that is sown.

The seed, described by Jesus as "the word of God" (verse 11), is the same in all four environments, but in only one case does the seed produce a lasting crop. This illustrates for us how important the soil is, because unless the Word of God has the right environment in order to produce growth, the growth you desire may not take place. Some Christians become frustrated that the Word of God is not working in their lives. However, the parable of the sower indicates that the deficiency is never in the seed (the Word of God), but in the receptivity of the soil and the life that it represents. The seed will never work until the deficiency of the soil is addressed.

Jesus closed this parable by calling out to the crowd gathered around Him, "He who has ears to hear, let him hear" (verse 8). What this means is that it is possible to have ears and hear the story without really hearing the meaning. The disciples followed up on Jesus' challenge to fully hear the meaning by asking Him to explain the particulars of the parable. In response, Jesus told them, "To you it has been granted to know the mysteries of the kingdom of God, but to the rest it is in parables, so that seeing they may not see, and hearing they may not understand" (verse 10).

The difference between the disciples and the rest of the crowd gathered around Jesus was that the disciples were not content with just a nice story. They wanted to know what the story meant for their own lives. This same difference is evident in many believers' lives today. In fact, many people show up to church to enjoy the music, programs, and sermons without pressing beyond the surface to apply the truth of Scripture to their everyday lives. Without application, they remain members of the crowd, not true disciples. Jesus described these individuals as seeing but not perceiving, hearing but not understanding (Mark 4:12 NIV).

The mystery of the parable is that the seed only grows in one soil. The seed must be nurtured, take root, and grow, and then it will produce fruit. In other words, the fruit of a growing, thriving Christian life never "just happens" by default. The point of conversion for every Christian is only the point of departure, and a true disciple must embark on a lifelong journey of cultivating the soil to produce the fruit of Christlikeness.

Through this parable, Jesus shared some common issues with

allowing the seed to grow in our lives. He compared these issues to what happens when seed is thrown on different kinds of soil.

A Hardened Heart

Jesus began explaining His parable with the seed sown on the roadside, which is not received because of a hardened heart (Luke 8:12). The wayside "soil" is ground that has not been tilled or prepared to receive the seed. It is the soil on which people walk or roll carts. As a result, the ground becomes packed down and hardened over the course of time. This soil represents the condition of an unsaved person whose heart is hardened and who refuses to hear and believe the Word of God.

In each of the other soil types in this parable (rocky, thorny, good), the seed is able to take root and grow in the believer's life. But in the roadside soil, the seed remains unburied—and as a result, "the birds of the air ate it up" (Luke 8:5). In John 12:24, Jesus told his disciples, "Truly, truly, I say to you, unless a grain of wheat falls into the earth and dies, it remains alone; but if it dies, it bears much fruit." For the seed of God's Word to produce fruit, it must fall into tilled ground, and it must be buried deep within the soil.

God will often use the circumstances of life to till and tear up hardened ground, and we must not resist the hand or the tools of the divine gardener in our lives or in the lives of those we love.

We discover in Luke 8 that the enemy of the seed is the devil himself. Jesus explained that the birds that come and eat up the unburied seed sown on the roadside soil represent the devil, who "comes and takes away the word from their heart" (verse 12). The devil is the enemy of the Word of God, and like a scavenging bird circling in the skies above, he is constantly on the alert for opportunities to steal the seed of God's Word before it can take root in a person's life.

As we've looked at before, John 10:10 warns us that the devil "comes only to steal and kill and destroy." One of the primary ways that the devil tries to prevent the Word of God from taking root is to challenge the truthfulness of that Word, just as he did in the garden with Eve. God had instructed Adam and Eve to abstain from only one tree in the garden, but the devil subtly challenged God's Word, twisting it to raise the question about the nature of God's goodness (Genesis 3:1-5).

In Mark's version of the parable of the sower, it's added that when Satan comes to steal the seed (the Word of God), he does so "immediately" (4:15). The reason for the devil's urgency in stealing the seed is to counteract the result of the seed when it takes root and begins to grow. The devil knows that the seed of God's Word will transform lives, and he will exert every effort and exploit every opportunity to steal the seed.

Shallow Roots

Another aspect that can stop the seed from growing in a person's life is rocky soil. Rocky soil hinders the seed from building a deep, sustaining root system (Luke 8:13). This soil represents a person who receives the Word of God with joy, and the seed begins to take root. The soil, however, is full of rocks, preventing the seed from putting down deep, firm roots. Thus, when trials or persecutions come, the initial growth from the seed withers because the shallow roots cannot sustain the life of the plant (verse 6).

Both Matthew and Mark's Gospels indicate that the presence of the Word of God is actually the reason for affliction and persecution in the life of an individual (Matthew 13:20-21; Mark 4:16-17). These verses reveal that the growth of the seed is only temporary; "then, when affliction or persecution arises because of the word, immediately they fall away" (Mark 4:17). This "affliction or persecution" is the conflict that arises when God's Word contradicts the ways of this world. The individual is then presented with a choice to follow God or follow the opinions of others. Because the Word of God has not taken root within the inner recesses of the person's heart and mind, they are not nurtured by its truth; therefore, "they believe for a while, and in time of temptation fall away" (Luke 8:13).

Distractions

In the third example given to us in this parable, the seed is sown on thorny ground. As a result, the seed and thorns grow together until the life of the plant is choked out by the presence of the thorns (Luke 8:7). These thorns were identified by Jesus as the "worries and riches and pleasures of this life" (verse 14). Thus, if the devil is unable to snatch the seed or make it wither by trials and afflictions, his method of choice to inhibit growth is distraction through the things of this world.

The point of Jesus' parables was to instruct the listeners in the mysteries of the eternal kingdom of God, which breaks into this world through the lives of those who believe, obey, and follow Jesus.

In the case of this thorny soil, the things of "this life" (worries, riches, and pleasures) become more important and more pressing than the things of the life to come. This truth is why our brief, passing life and the temptations that accompany it must be contextualized within the perspective of the eternal kingdom-life that Jesus came to offer. When we become overly concerned with buying items we do not need with money we do not have to impress people we do not know, the thorns of this life will choke out the spiritual growth and fruitfulness that the seed was designed to produce.

A Humble Response

Yet when the seed is allowed to take root, it can produce great fruit in your life (i.e., spiritual growth, Christlikeness, and an impact on the lives of others). In each of the other soil types, the seed as the Word of God is heard, but it is not able to thrive and produce fruit. The difference in this fourth and final soil is that the Word of God is heard and held fast with an "honest and good heart" (Luke 8:15). When the Word of God is heard, it calls forth a response of repentance and obedience from the hearer. The Word must be tightly embraced so it can bring about change in your life. Without this honest and humble response, the seed of the Word of God remains outside the realities of your fallen, sinful self, and it is unable to put down roots in your soul that can lead to transformation and an intimate, experiential knowledge of God.

What often prevents this response of repentance and change in our lives, though, is that when we receive God's perspective on a matter through His Word, we mix His wisdom with the opinions of others around us—and our own opinions as well. Amid this cacophony, we become like a television with a bad receiver. The Word of God that confronts our lives becomes lost within the static of other voices, including our own.

Yet, when the seed is held fast, the Word of God then bears fruit within the life of the believer (Luke 8:15). Once the soil has been tilled and cultivated by the repentance and obedience that comes from an "honest and good heart," the seed can begin to do its work of transformation. There is no miraculous shortcut or quick-growth formula for the seed of the Word of God. Its presence in your life must be real and impacting so that, with the perseverance of abiding in its truth, it is able to put down deep roots in the soil of your life.

James 1:25 states it this way: "One who looks intently at the perfect law, the law of liberty, and abides by it, not having become a forgetful hearer but an effectual doer, this man will be blessed in what he does." The Word of God must be looked at intently, and its truth must be obeyed before it can bear the fruit that it was designed to produce. In other words, when the Word of God is read, meditated upon, memorized, and lived out, the seed will find good, cultivated soil—soil that "produce[s] a crop a hundred times as great" (Luke 8:8). Without this, the identity of the divine nature within you will remain dormant and will fail to impact or benefit you in any significant way on earth.

It is only in the application of biblical truth to your everyday life, thoughts, decisions, and viewpoint that you discover the benefits of this divine nature within you and come to know your true identity. Seek to apply God's Word to every aspect of your life, and in so doing, you will discover the fullness and abundance of life Jesus came to supply.

12

EXPERIENCING FRUITFULNESS

God illustrates the product of knowing Him fully with the concept of "fruit." Fruit is God's spiritual reference to what our lives produce when our character reflects His. Galatians 5:22-24 speaks explicitly of this fruit.

> The fruit of the Spirit is love, joy, peace, patience, kindness, goodness, faithfulness, gentleness, self-control; against such things there is no law. Now those who belong to Christ Jesus have crucified the flesh with its passions and desires.

No other place in Scripture lays out the attributes of the character of God so clearly. If you want evidence that you are deepening in your intimate relationship with God, just look at what a life present with Christ and filled by the Holy Spirit produces. The results include character qualities that reflect God Himself. But more than that, they also include an increase of productivity in your work and advancement of God's kingdom agenda on earth. God created you to maximize your productivity for Him through your connection to Him.

In business, we would call this "generating a healthy return on investment." In sports, it's known as a winning game or season. In music, it's a platinum album. And in your personal life, producing fruit means leveraging everything at your disposal for the glory of God and the betterment of yourself and others. This even applies to what you choose to think and say: "Through Him then, let us continually offer up a sacrifice of praise to God, that is, the fruit of lips that give thanks to His name" (Hebrews 13:15).

As we saw in a previous chapter, fruit has three distinct characteristics: visibility, authenticity, and availability. You've never seen nor eaten invisible fruit. You've never gone shopping for invisible fruit. Fruit—be it an orange, pear, apple, or banana—is always something you see. Similarly, if knowing God produces results that are not visible to others—or even to yourself—then there's not much of a relationship there at all. Fruit is always visible.

Secondly, fruit always bears the character of the tree from which it came. You won't find pears on apple trees or oranges on pear trees. This is because fruit authentically replicates the nature of the tree.

When a believer resembles anything other than the character and qualities of God, they are not relationally attached to God. Yes, they may be eternally saved through Christ's atonement on the cross, but their soul has neglected the process of being sanctified here on earth.

For example, if a person reflects the values of their culture, then their culture is the source they tap into. If a combination of the values of your culture, entertainment, self-interests, and your social circle are reflected in your thoughts, words, and actions, then those are the things to which you are attached. This is because fruit authentically resembles what it is attached to the most.

Lastly, fruit never exists for itself. Fruit is always available for the consumption of someone else. The only fruit you ever see eating itself is rotten fruit. Think about it: When fruit is rotten, it begins a process of eating away at its own existence, shriveling into a shell of its once wondrous beginnings. Fruit exists so that someone else can bite it, be nourished by it, enjoy it, and grow from it.

God desires for you to know Him in many ways in order to bear much fruit. How do I know that? Because Jesus tells us in John 15:16,

> You did not choose Me but I chose you, and appointed you that you would go and bear fruit, and that your fruit would remain, so that whatever you ask of the Father in My name He may give to you.

You have been chosen to be productive. You have been appointed to maximize your spiritual potential. You have been created to nourish and delight others through the gifts, skills, time, and talents the Lord has placed in you. Your calling to live as a full-on, fire-breathing, sold-out, sanctified child of the King has nothing to do with where you came from or what family you were born into. God isn't looking for a certain pedigree when it comes to you being used by Him to feed, equip, and strengthen others. He has a purpose for you, and that purpose belongs only to you. You are to bear fruit that will last. You are to leave a legacy.

NO FORCED FRUIT

So how do you go about this process of bearing fruit as a believer in Christ since it is what Jesus desires of you? Is there a special formula? Does it require an extreme amount of effort? Does it happen when you wake at a certain hour or cross off a list of tasks that you think will make you a successful kingdom disciple? Does it mean going to church whenever the doors are open or volunteering whenever someone is needed?

You may be surprised to discover that bearing fruit takes a different type of effort.

Have you ever seen a pear or an apple struggling and straining to become a pear or an apple? Or how about grapes on a vine? No, none of us have ever seen that. This is because the simple act of abiding brings about the growth of the fruit. It is in your closeness to Christ that fruit is created both in and through your life.

Paul gives us insight into how our relationship with God determines our productivity for God when he says, "We have not ceased to pray for you and to ask that you may be filled with the knowledge of His will in all spiritual wisdom and understanding, so that you will walk in a manner worthy of the Lord, to please Him in all respects, bearing fruit in every good work and increasing in the knowledge of God" (Colossians 1:9-10). In this passage there is a direct connection between bearing fruit and knowing God.

The Greek word for *knowledge* in these verses is *epignosis*. It means "precise and correct knowledge."[3] But what does it mean to have such knowledge of God? Well, this is what we typically think:

> *To know God means you should...*
> *read your Bible.*
> *recite a verse a day to keep the devil away.*
> *go to church.*
> *say a prayer.*
> *take an online course on Scripture or theology.*

That's usually how we interpret what it means to know God. And that's also why so few of us truly live out the full manifestation of His fruit in and through our lives. To know God goes much deeper than informational knowledge alone. It's not just about content. It's about so much more.

In chapter 1 we read about another instance of a word we translate as *knowing*: "Adam knew Eve his wife; and she conceived, and bare Cain" (Genesis 4:1 KJV). The word *knew* in this verse is the Hebrew word *yada*, which means "to know" and "to know by experience" and "to perceive."[4] When Adam knew Eve, it didn't mean he had information about her. No, it meant so much more.

In other words, there was a level of intimacy between them that produced fruit. It bore new life.

To know someone encompasses more than just knowing about them. To truly know someone involves an engagement, interaction, intimacy, and understanding that goes above and beyond cognitive realities. Have you ever seen dancers who spend hours upon hours, days, weeks, and months practicing together so that they know each other's moves and moods through being close to each other? They can anticipate the next step and know how to bring out the best in their dancing partner.

The best linebackers in the NFL are those who have worked so closely together that they can predict each other's moves simply through a shift in weight or a change in the placement of a hand. With crowds roaring and tensions high, these linemen don't have time to talk to the other linemen to find out what they are thinking. But the best players can intuit what their teammates are going to do because they know them that well.

When the apostle Paul talks about knowing God, he's talking about entering into an experiential connection with God. He's talking about knowing Him so deeply, fully, continually, intentionally, and relationally that your every move aligns with His in a cadence of connection. That's what it means to know God. And when you know Him at that level, fruit will be produced. You won't have to force it or fake it; you'll just create it. Or rather, it will be created in you.

It is in God that you are supplied with all the wisdom you need to walk in the work He has for you to do, to bear fruit (Colossians 1:9-10). God longs to produce something in you that is beautiful and enjoyable—fruit of impact, influence, and usefulness. God desires that your experience of knowing Him gives birth to luscious fruit in your character, conduct, and contributions. But friend, that only comes about through intimacy with God Himself—through truly knowing Him.

ABIDING

This is what Paul urges us toward in knowing God. Our experience with God is to be so rich and deep that we cannot help but bear fruit. And the only way that is done is through a process called "abiding." We learn about this process in John 15, where Jesus says,

> I am the true vine, and My Father is the vinedresser. Every branch in Me that does not bear fruit, He takes away; and every branch that bears fruit, He prunes it so that it may bear more fruit. You are already clean because of the word which I have spoken to you. Abide in Me, and I in you. As the branch cannot bear fruit of itself unless it abides in the vine, so neither can you unless you abide in Me. I am the vine, you are the branches; he who abides in Me and I in him, he bears much fruit, for apart from Me you can do nothing (verses 1-5).

Here's the picture Jesus paints for us: There is a great vineyard, a vine, a gardener, and branches that either bear fruit or do not. God is the gardener; Christ is the vine. You are a branch. Every branch that abides in Christ bears fruit. In fact, they bear *much* fruit. Conversely, no branch can bear fruit in and of itself. If a branch lacks an abiding presence in the vine, it also lacks fruit. Spiritual truths rarely come simpler than this one.

Hang out with (abide in) Christ, and you will bear fruit.

Live apart from Christ, and you will not bear fruit.

Your fruit bearing is entirely dependent on your relational intimacy with Jesus Christ and His written Word. You can't skip that reality. You can't force fruit to grow. You can't even study it into existence. Fruit bearing all comes down to one very critical, yet also very simple, condition: abiding in Jesus Christ. This principle is so important that the word *abide* shows up ten times in only six verses from John 15.

> "Abide in Me" (verse 4).
>
> "Unless it abides in the vine" (verse 4).
>
> "Unless you abide in Me" (verse 4).
>
> "He who abides in Me" (verse 5).
>
> "If anyone does not abide in Me" (verse 6).
>
> "If you abide in Me" (verse 7).
>
> "My words abide in you" (verse 7).
>
> "Abide in My love" (verse 9).
>
> "You will abide in My love" (verse 10).
>
> "Abide in His love" (verse 10).

Evidently, Jesus really wants us to know about abiding! The sole purpose of the branch is to abide in the vine. So what does it look like to abide in Christ? Well, we can start to understand this by discovering what it looks like to abide somewhere else.

A number of years ago, my wife and I took a trip to the great grape-growing countryside in Napa Valley, California. People come from all over America—and even from all around the world—to taste wine and see the miles and miles of vines blanketing the hills in sweet scents.

One thing you will always see in a vineyard are the branches hoisted up and tied to posts so that the grapes don't drag on the ground. If the grapes drag on the ground, they will never grow properly; they will become stuck in the dirt, unable to absorb any sunlight or receive a steady flow of nutrients. So the gardeners gently lift the grapes off the ground so that they can grow to their full potential.

One reason so many people fail to produce fruit in their lives is because they spend too much time settling in and around too much dirt. See, a lot of believers say, "God, make me fruitful," but He will not do it because they don't want to be taken away from the dirt. You must address unaddressed sin in your life if God is going to be free to lift you up and out of the mire. You can't hang out in the dirt and also get the sunshine—those two options are mutually exclusive.

Regardless of that reality, the dirt beckons more people away from their full expression than you may realize. Whether it's to numb feelings of loneliness, rejection, inadequacy, or fears of the future, many seem to have a predilection toward activities that provide a distraction rather than produce development.

Another fruit-related description for these distractions is "sucker shoots."

Not all hindrances to producing fruit occur in the dirt. Some of these hindrances come from things that are seemingly good and beneficial. That's why the illustration given to us in John 15 goes into greater detail. We read, "Every branch in Me that does not bear fruit, He takes away; and every branch that bears fruit, He prunes it so that it may bear more fruit" (verse 2). Pruning is cutting away that which siphons off life.

Suckers are little branches that show up on the vine and take away some of the nutrients designed to help the fruit expand to its fullest potential. Simply put, a sucker is a diversion. It doesn't produce anything in and of itself. It just hangs out near the nutrients with no intention of developing anything from the nutrients it consumes. A sucker takes from you what belongs to you, thus limiting what you need for fruit bearing. It siphons off what is there to keep you flowing Godward.

In our personal lives, anyone or anything can be a sucker, be it a person, the television, or a hobby. And while there may be nothing wrong with that person, TV show, or hobby, when it starts to rob you of what you need to develop your spiritual intimacy with Jesus, it has transitioned into a sucker. That's why the concept of moderation is so important. You have to create boundaries in your life in order to allow yourself the opportunity to abide.

Abiding requires time. It requires repeat exposure. Consider the two types of tea drinkers. Some people like to dip their tea bag up and down in the hot water because they don't want their tea to get too strong. Others drop the tea bag in and just leave it there. That way the hot water can fully absorb all that the tea bag has to offer.

When a tea bag abides in hot water, the tea becomes strong.

When you abide in Jesus Christ, your spiritual power, insight, and development become strong. You grow. Just like a baby in a mother's womb who gets his or her nutrients through the umbilical cord, the abiding connection produces growth. If there were to be a breach in the umbilical cord, there would also be a shrinking of life itself. It is the ongoing connection with the mother that keeps the baby growing and developing.

If you have ever dated someone you fell in love with, then you need no further illustration of what it means to abide. A text message here, phone call there, time spent together, and so on. When people date, they don't just connect once a week for a few hours and then are done with it. In fact, when two people are deeply in love, they will abide in each other's presence on the phone way past the point when there is anything meaningful left to say. They simply don't want to hang up. And then, as soon as they do, one of them will text how much they are missing the other.

We know that is true in relationships, yet we often fail to transfer that reality to our relationship with Jesus Christ. Far too many believers assume that a two-hour visit on Sunday morning is enough. Or perhaps they add on a Wednesday-night appearance, a verse in the morning, or a quick prayer when trouble pops up. But try applying the way you relate to Jesus to how you relate to other people in your life and see what happens. You might just lose a few friends and family members. Try making every single conversation you have with a romantic partner, family member, or even a friend about you and what you want them to do for you, and you might find yourself alone very quickly. But that's what most people do with Christ. They toss up a quick prayer, a wish list of sorts, and then wonder why they are living such a fruitless, powerless, empty life.

Jesus wants a relationship, not your religious activity. Sometimes that will involve a five-second prayer just to let Him know you are thinking about Him. Other times it could be a five-minute prayer. Sometimes it will be deep. Other times it will be light. But the essence of abiding is that you are threading Jesus Christ (His presence, desires, and thoughts) through all you think, do, and say. As 1 Corinthians 10:31 says, "Whether, then, you eat or drink or whatever you do, do all to the glory of God."

What too many people want is a microwave experience of God, when God is offering a Crock-Pot experience. They want to go to church and push a button for some quick results. But the truth about microwaved food is that it can get real hot real quick, but then it can get real cold real quick. That's because the food hasn't abided in the presence of that which heats it.

It is in the abiding that you will discover the fruit.

Which is why knowing God is the key to experiencing a greater level of spiritual growth, development, and productivity. In fact, the busier you are, the more important it is to carve out time to abide with Christ. Yes, you may feel busy and overwhelmed, and your schedule might support those feelings. But look at the gaps that life gives you as gifts to cultivate your abiding relationship with Jesus Christ. Seize those moments and guard them fiercely. He is worth it. You are worth it. And the fruit that is produced both in and through you is worth it.

Don't waste your life in a perpetual state of busyness, seeking to fill the gaps in your day with suckers or distractions. Rather, embrace the gaps life has to offer and discover unimagined depths in knowing God.

He longs for you to know Him that way. He longs for your company, your voice, your presence, and your conversations. The fruit will come—but it will only come as a by-product of tapping into and staying connected with Jesus Christ. This, and this alone, enables your character to reflect His heart in every way, shape, and form.

13

EXPERIENCING PURPOSE

The foundational principle for your purpose is this: God created you for Himself. Which is why knowing God intimately is foundational for the fulfillment of your purpose.

You were created for God. You weren't created for yourself.

You were not created so that God can spend all His time trying to figure out how to help you out. God created you for the purpose He has for you—to accomplish His plan for the advancement of His kingdom and for His glory. Any other foundation than this will take you anywhere else but the fulfillment of your purpose.

Scripture tells us that "Enoch walked with God" (Genesis 5:24), not that God walked with Enoch. God is not your copilot; He is in charge. First Corinthians 8:6 states, "For us there is but one God, the Father, from whom are all things and we exist for Him; and one Lord, Jesus Christ, by whom are all things, and we exist through Him."

You exist for God's purposes. Your purpose is His purpose. The Bible doesn't open with, "In the beginning you..." The Bible opens with, "In the beginning God..." (Genesis 1:1). God is the beginning.

The book of Colossians goes deeper into this foundational truth.

> By Him all things were created, both in the heavens and on earth, visible and invisible, whether thrones or dominions or rulers or authorities—all things have been created through Him and for Him. He is before all things, and in Him all things hold together (1:16-17).

Notice that Scripture does not say, "All things have been created through Him and for you." God created all things through Him and for *Him*. That includes you. You have been created for God Himself.

Not only that, but we saw that God is "before all things" as well. He is first. Having a purpose-filled life is all about proper alignment. When God is positioned first in your life, then the next part of that verse holds true for you: "In Him all things hold together."

So if you are unraveling—or if you lack peace, security, stability, and purpose—the first thing you need to ask is what position you are giving God in your life. Because if He is truly before all things in your life, then all things in your life will be held together by Him.

But if He is not before all things, then you cannot expect all things to be held together by Him. God has to be positioned *before* all things in order for those things to be held together.

THE CENTRAL FOCUS

Why do so many people struggle with stability, calm, and peace and so frequently face a life of emotional, spiritual, or even physical chaos? The answer is simple. Because God has not been positioned before all things for them. He is not first. Instead, He is "in addition to" all things. Or perhaps He comes after trying other things. Yet God will only hold the plan of your life together when He is before all things in your life.

The apostle Paul sheds more light on this in Ephesians, where we read,

> He made known to us the mystery of His will, according to His kind intention which He purposed in Him with a view to an administration suitable to the fullness of the times, that is, the summing up of all things in Christ, things in the heavens and things on the earth. In Him also we have obtained an inheritance, having been predestined according to His purpose who works all things after the counsel of His will (1:9-11).

God desires to know you deeply, not just because you will go to heaven one day, but because He wants to fulfill His purpose through you on earth. Don't misinterpret what this means. God *does* want to empower you. But He wants to empower you in line with His purpose, not in line with your desires outside of His purpose and intention for your life. If you are living outside of God's purpose, then you are living outside of the full realization of His power in your life to fulfill that purpose. You are living without experiencing God's reality within you to the maximum potential because you are living outside of the foundational starting point for your life.

In the Old Testament, we read about the life of God's servant David. While David was not a perfect man, he was referred to in Scripture as a man after God's own heart (1 Samuel 13:14; Acts 13:22). David probably knew God better than most people who have ever lived. In the book of Acts, we discover what knowing God and being a man after God's own heart is all about: "David, after he had served the purpose of God in his own generation, fell asleep, and was laid among his fathers" (13:36).

David was a man who was about more than just church attendance, Bible reading and memorization, committee membership, and dancing in the street. David was a man after God's purpose.

David's biblical epitaph tells us a lot by what it does not say. We do not read,

> "David, after he had become the head of the company..."
>
> "David, after he had made so much money..."
>
> "David, after he had won so many battles..."
>
> "David, after he had risen in his social circles..."
>
> "David, after he had purchased lots of brand-name clothes..."

Instead we read, "David, after he had served the purpose of God..."
That's what it means to be a man or woman after God's own heart.
That's what it means to know God and experience the power of knowing Him. David did what he had been put on earth to do. He knew
that it wasn't about him. He hadn't bought into the "Bless Me Movement" that tends to view God as a cosmic vending machine where you
put in your coins and push the buttons, and He dispenses what you
want. David realized that God's blessings are tied to God's purpose.

For thousands of years, many people believed that the sun and
planets revolved around the earth. But in the sixteenth century, Pol-
ish astronomer Nicolaus Copernicus published a treatise that presented a heliocentric model for our galaxy. Up until then, the earth
was mostly viewed as the central point for all else.

What was once done astronomically, a lot of believers have done
philosophically and psychologically. They have gotten it all wrong.
They view themselves as the central point of life around which all
other things, including God, are to revolve. In fact, this has become
such a prominent belief system in these latter days that we are close
to falling into what could be considered a narcissistic epidemic.

But this view is not God's. God says He is the center around
which we are to revolve. He is the focal point. He holds all things
together.

If you truly want to discover and live out God's purpose for
your life, you will need to switch your thinking from seeing God as
a vending machine to seeing Him as the central focus of your life.

When a woman gives birth to a baby, she is the one who must
adjust to the baby. In order to fully nourish and cherish the new life

she has been given, her sleeping schedule must adjust. Her daily plans must adjust. Her priorities must adjust.

New life means adjustment.

The new life that you received when you were saved ought to have created an adjustment in your perspective, planning, and priorities as well. If it didn't, then you are still living for yourself. You are still focused on knowing yourself. You are still seeing yourself as the center of your universe, rather than being focused on God's intentions for you.

When someone finds out they have cancer, that is a bad situation—because the cancer takes over. Cancer wouldn't be so bad if it would just show up and stay still.

We often want God to do what we want cancer to do: show up and stay still. We'll schedule Him in for a few hours on Sunday. During the week, we'll possibly say a few prayers and maybe read a devotional book or even a couple chapters of the Bible. We might toss Him into a few of our conversations. But when it comes to God actually taking over, that's not how we roll. We have our own purpose for our time, talents, and treasures. And because of that, we will often face a life of emptiness or chaos. If we would only yield to God and His purposes, we would see the miracles that He can make out of what looks to be a mess. We would witness His power as He brings us to the fulfillment of our purpose and the restoration of our lost hope.

A HOPEFUL FUTURE

I have talked with a number of people over the years who seem to be living with a sense of hopelessness. Questions bounce around in their heads, such as, *Am I ever going to get where I am supposed to be? Am I ever going to do what I am supposed to do? Is life ever going to work for me?* They have lost a sense of purpose. What's more, they have lost a sense of hope.

Friend, if that sounds like you, I have a verse to encourage you on your journey. In fact, it is a positive verse located in the middle of a negative chapter that is located within a negative book. It is a ray of hope surrounded by a series of discouragements.

Perhaps that is how you feel today. You may feel like you are surrounded by bad day after bad day. Or perhaps it's been bad year after bad year, or even bad decade after bad decade. Yet, even though this verse is situated in the middle of desperation and hopeless scenarios, it offers hope, meaning, and purpose. You, too, can discover the power to carry out your purpose even in the midst of despair.

> "I know the plans that I have for you," declares the Lord, "plans for welfare and not for calamity to give you a future and a hope" (Jeremiah 29:11).

That is God's promise for you. That is what you can count on when you draw near to Him to get to know Him fully. After all, He follows up that verse with the formula toward its attainment. Notice how it involves calling on Him, seeking Him, and searching for Him. In other words, knowing Him.

> "Then you will call upon Me and come and pray to Me, and I will listen to you. You will seek Me and find *Me* when you search for Me with all your heart. I will be found by you," declares the Lord" (verses 12-14).

God says that when we seek Him, He will allow Himself to be found and, as a result, He will fulfill His promises of restoration, purpose, and hope (verse 14).

New Year's resolutions: Many of us make them, and most of us break them. They cover everything from being a better person to eating healthier, working out at the gym, memorizing Scripture, and watching less football. The simplest definition of a resolution is "a firm decision to do or not to do something."[5]

In January, our resolutions resound with determination, offering the potential of new beginnings. By May, most of those resolutions will merely remind us through their nagging presence that we didn't quite reach our goals. By December, the majority of us will have forgotten what we had once resolved to do.

Whether or not you join with the millions in making New Year's resolutions, I want to remind you that there is one who has kept every resolution He has ever made. He keeps His promises. He keeps His Word. "He who promised is faithful" (Hebrews 10:23).

Even if we are not able to stick it out at the gym, stay away from the chocolate, or bite our tongue rather than beat others with it, God is "able to do far more abundantly beyond all that we ask or think" (Ephesians 3:20). And He has resolved that your life is going to be a *great* life—a life on purpose, one filled with both "a future and a hope" (Jeremiah 29:11). The surest way to live out your purpose is to fix your eyes on the unchanging faithfulness of the one who has promised that goodness and lovingkindness will follow you when you follow Him (Psalm 23:6).

Your life may hold some surprises, but I know who holds your life. And He says that you are to "be of good cheer," because He has already overcome it all (John 16:33 KJV). If He has overcome it, then you have overcome it as His child and heir.

I understand how easy it is to get caught up in the circumstances of life. They can seem overwhelming. I also understand how easy it is to lose hope. But if you will keep your eyes fixed on the Lord—and not on your circumstances—you will see that "He who began a good work in you" will also complete it (Philippians 1:6).

People lose hope when they can't see a future. They know that yesterday was bleak, today is bleak, and tomorrow doesn't look any better. The weather report of their lives says, "No sunshine." There seems to be nothing out there related to their calling or destiny.

If you are one of those people, you need to memorize and meditate on Jeremiah 29:11. This great verse is for anyone who feels that they have a bad life. In it, God spoke hope to the Israelites while they were still in captivity in Babylon.

Jeremiah 29:4 tells us, "Thus says the LORD of hosts, the God of Israel, to all the exiles whom I have sent into exile from Jerusalem to Babylon." The Israelites had been sent into exile. They were under God's judgment and His disciplining hand for an extended period of time.

To make it worse, the place where they had been sent was as pagan as you could get. Babylon is not where the God followers hung out. It was an evil and idolatrous place; a terrible place to live, particularly if you were an Israelite. These people were in a desperate situation full of negative circumstances laden with divine discipline in a pagan environment. Yet, in the midst of this discouragement, hopelessness, and pain, God showed up and said, "I know the plans that I have for you" (verse 11).

Why is that so important? Because when God says He has a plan, you know the story's not over. In fact, if you are still here, then you can assume that your life is not over. Your destiny is not over. Your purpose is not over. Your calling is not over. If you are still living, breathing, and functioning on Planet Earth, God has a plan just for you.

You may be thinking, *But Tony, you don't know about my past. My past is messed up—God would never use me.* Well, Israel had a past too. Yet God still had a plan for them that included "a future and a hope."

Remember, some of your greatest lessons on faith and humility will be learned in the dark. These are the times when you feel so hopeless that you don't know what in the world God is doing, how He is doing it, and why it is taking so long. But when God is silent, He is not still. When you feel furthest from Him, He is the closest He'll ever be. One of the key components to living a life of power is learning how to trust the Lord in times that don't make sense.

I know there are times when your life may look dark or seem unclear, and you have no idea where God is taking you. In fact, it may be pitch-black outside. But if you are in one of those times right now, hold on—because when God moves, you will move. I don't know why He has you stuck, delayed, or seemingly hindered from living out your purpose right at this very moment. But I do know this: He has a plan for you, and it is a good plan to give you both "a future and a hope."

IN THE MEANTIME

God tells you what to do while you are waiting for the timing of your purpose to come about, just like He told the Israelites. Earlier in Jeremiah 29, He instructed them, "Build houses and live in them; and plant gardens and eat their produce...Seek the welfare of the city where I have sent you into exile, and pray to the LORD on its behalf; for in its welfare you will have welfare" (verses 5,7).

Waiting on the timing of your purpose does not mean that you sit back and just do nothing. God says to become as productive as you possibly can where you are. Do all that is in your hand to do. Maximize everything that is set before you. Seize the opportunities where you are.

One of the primary things you can do while waiting on God is promote the well-being of those around you. Even if you are not in a location where you want to be or if you are not doing what you want to do, benefit those around you. Invest in them and increase their well-being. Surely the Israelites were not happy about their captivity in Babylon, but God instructed them not only to pray for the betterment of the Babylonians, but also to tangibly seek that betterment through their actions. He told them that in the Babylonians' well-being they would find their own. God would bless them for being a blessing to others.

Many of us choose to do nothing while waiting on God to bring a change in our lives or to get us out of a situation we don't like. But there is only one time when you are to do nothing, and that is when there is nothing to do. If there is nothing you can do, then do nothing. But if God has given you something that you can do where you are right now, "do it with all your might" (Ecclesiastes 9:10). Invest in your surroundings. Seek the well-being of those around you. As you become a blessing to others, you are setting yourself up to be blessed. As you help others locate and live out their destinies, you are setting yourself up to discover your own.

One of the main reasons people lose hope is because they are only concerned about themselves. If your life is messed up and all you can see is yourself, then you are perpetuating your own demise. In spite of the Israelites' circumstances, they were to be productive on behalf of others. They were to invest in the lives of others. As a result, God promised to invest in their own lives as well.

Many Christians read and quote Jeremiah 29:11 without fully understanding the context of the verse. As a result, the principles in the surrounding verses are often thrown out, making verse 11 fail to come to pass. It is in the context of pursuing and knowing God that the promise is set.

Rather than search for God with all our heart, as it says in verse 13, we search for meaning or the solutions to our problems with all our heart. We search for the wrong thing, and so we don't find it. God says that He has the plan. He has *your* plan. He doesn't want you to go looking for the plan; He wants you to go searching for Him. When you find Him, you will also find the plan, because He knows what it is.

God has a plan for you. Prioritizing knowing Him will bring about the revelation of that plan. Yes, maybe you should have gotten this earlier in your life. Maybe you shouldn't have done this, that, or the other that got you off track. Or maybe if someone else wouldn't have done something to you, you would have understood earlier. If you had been saved sooner, if you hadn't married that person or sought that career outside of God's will, or if you hadn't just been plain rebellious—maybe you would have reached your purpose before now. Regardless, God has a plan for you. And if you're still here, He still wants you to live it.

It wound up being 70 years before Israel got to see God's plan. The prophets were falsely telling them about their deliverance (Jeremiah 14:13-14; 29:8-9). But the false prophets didn't know. They just told the people what they wanted to hear. God knew the exile would be longer than they thought. That's why He told them to be as productive as they could be in the place where they were until they saw Him do what He said He would do.

The Israelites didn't like being in bondage. Just like I'm sure you don't like being in the dark about your own purpose and future. But Scripture tells us that "without faith it is impossible to please [God], for he who comes to God must believe that He is and that He is a rewarder of those who seek Him" (Hebrews 11:6).

It all boils down to knowing God. Knowing Him deeply. Knowing Him continually. Knowing Him passionately. Knowing Him authentically. Knowing Him fully. The power of knowing God is unleashed in the knowledge of Him.

If you don't know which way to go in your life, seek Him.

If you are in pain, seek Him.

If you are confused, seek Him.

If you are waiting, seek Him.

If you track me down and ask me which way you are supposed

to go, I'm going to send you back to God, because He has not told me His plan for you. You need to seek Him and know Him in order to discover the pathway to your purpose.

Sometimes it will look like God is doing nothing. Oftentimes, actually. Yet God often works behind the scenes in ways that you cannot see in order to take yesterday's pains and turn them into tomorrow's peace. God is asking you to take hold of His hand and never let it go because He knows where He is taking you. It is a good, wonderful place because it has "a future and a hope." What God starts, He finishes. What God begins, He ends. What God initiates, He completes. But you may think, *Tony, I'm in a mess right now, and you don't know my mess.* To which I reply, "Then you don't know my God."

He's bigger than your mess.

Now, if you forget everything else you've read in this book so far, remember this one thing that God says: "I know the plans that I have for you...plans for welfare and not for calamity to give you a future and a hope" (Jeremiah 29:11).

He knows the plans.

He knows your purpose.

You access both by knowing Him more fully, the one who knows everything there is to know about you—past, present, and future.

14

EXPERIENCING COMMUNITY

I love to watch the Olympics. Not only do these two weeks bring us a wide variety of sports to observe, but they also give us the opportunity to take part in others' successes. While we viewers never have to get up at 4:00 a.m. to work out or devote our time, lifestyle, and eating habits to winning a gold medal, we do get to feel the emotions of those who come out on top. It's powerful to watch the athletes stand on the podium—often with tears streaming down their faces—and receive the medal they so feverishly strived to achieve.

Recently, a member of the church I pastor won the gold medal in her sport. It was the first gold medal ever won in her event for an American. Watching someone I had known from her childhood onward climb atop that stand and claim the highest award in the world in her sport filled my own heart with a sense of accomplishment and joy. Hers was an individual sport. Her medal didn't come tied to a group effort or team attempt. It was her individual skill, power, determination, commitment, and ability that grabbed her the gold.

Yet, when she stood on the platform that day, they didn't ask her, "What's your favorite song so we can play it?" No, they played the national anthem of the United States of America, because it was understood that while an individual won the event, she represented something much bigger in winning it.

Similarly, if you head to any city where their team recently won the Super Bowl or World Series and listen to the fans, you won't hear them talking about the team that won the trophy. No, you'll hear such things as, "We won!" or, "We are the champions!" Granted, these fans never spent a second on the field or in the gym in pursuit of that victory, but they claim it just the same. This is because it is understood that there exists an integral connection between the individual accomplishments of a team and the collective impact on the city that team represents. There is a sense that the city participated experientially in the win by virtue of the relationship.

THE DIVIDING WALL

In coming to know God personally, a key component of His nature calls for our attention. It's not something we are unaware of, but its practical implications are often left out. That component is this: God exists in both the one and the many. There is only one God, but we also know that He consists of three coequal persons: God the Father, God the Son, and God the Holy Spirit. Each is unique in their personhood and personality, yet unified in their essence and purpose. They function as one, even though they carry out distinct roles. We refer to the unity of the Godhead as the Trinity.

Thus, the greatness of God is not merely in His singularity, but also in His collectivity.

As an individual believer pursuing knowledge of God, you need to know that you can experience God to a point on your own. He expects you to grow in your faith and maturity as an individual. However, there are some aspects of experiencing and knowing God that you will never gain outside of a connection with other people in His body. It is only as you are connected to His people and His collective purposes that He will enable you to see things you would never see in your private Christian experience. There are many great and wonderful blessings that God supplies to a group of believers when they are rightly unified.

There is no such thing as a lone-ranger Christian, nor does God have any only children. Yet I'm concerned that our me-focused, autonomous culture falls short in knowing God and experiencing Him collectively. And while an emphasis on individuality in our nation is not all bad, it can encourage believers to carry that emphasis too far in their spiritual walk. With this emphasis, a person can easily forget about God's collective program and their participation in it. What's more, they may be suffering the implications of being disconnected from the body of Christ while not even being aware of the cause of the consequences in their life.

The book of Ephesians is my favorite New Testament book. When Paul penned this book, he was addressing the needs of the church. And one of the problems Paul had to address was conflict in the church. There existed an ethnic divide between Jews and Gentiles set entirely on culture, not biblical beliefs. Essentially, two groups of people just couldn't get along.

Knowing this divide would lead to fissions and fractures in God's overarching kingdom agenda on earth, Paul urged the believers in Ephesus to remove the line between them. In Ephesians 2:14 he wrote, "[Christ] himself is our peace, who has made the two groups one and has destroyed the barrier, the dividing wall of hostility" (NIV).

Paul was writing at a time when many would understand the reference to a "dividing wall." There was a wall erected in the temple, and the Gentiles were not permitted to go beyond it. It was a division set up to separate the Jews from the Gentiles within the temple. Paul was pointing out through his statements made in Ephesians that such division no longer existed. Once Jesus Christ came on the scene, He tore down that wall.

Perhaps you remember the iconic scene from the late 1980s when President Ronald Reagan spoke poetically and powerfully to the leader of the Soviet Union, one of the most powerful nations in the world, and said, "Mr. Gorbachev, tear down this wall!" President Reagan was referencing the dividing wall that had stood between West and East Germany since 1961. This wall not only divided two groups of people from associating with one another, but it also dictated what kind of life each person could pursue, depending on which side of the wall they lived. In seeking equity, justice, and peace, a long line of discussions and negotiations had taken place regarding removal of the dividing wall. Ultimately, in 1989, it came down in dramatic form with large chunks falling symbolically to the ground.

This visual helps us understand more fully the dividing wall that had been in place between the Jews (God's chosen people) and the Gentiles, up through the time of Jesus Christ. Division existed on all levels, but primarily spiritually. Yet when Jesus came, He ushered in a season of unity and equity for all. His death positioned us equally at the foot of His cross. Not only did Jesus die to offer salvation to all mankind, but He also provided the opportunity for humans to remove the hostility between one another.

> He himself is our peace, who has made the two groups one and has destroyed the barrier, the dividing wall of hostility, by setting aside in his flesh the law with its commands and regulations. His purpose was to create in himself one new humanity out of the two, thus making peace, and in one body to reconcile both of them to God through the cross, by which he put to death their hostility. He came and preached peace to you who were far away and peace to those who were near. For through him we both have access to the Father by one Spirit.

> Consequently, you are no longer foreigners and strangers, but fellow citizens with God's people and also members of his household, built on the foundation of the apostles and prophets, with Christ Jesus

himself as the chief cornerstone. In him the whole building is joined together and rises to become a holy temple in the Lord. And in him you too are being built together to become a dwelling in which God lives by his Spirit (Ephesians 2:14-22 NIV).

You are part of something bigger than your own personal experience. We are explicitly told that God's direct purpose in sending His Son, Jesus Christ, was to reconcile all of humanity not only to Himself, but also to one another. He set about to erase the hostility between us, making peace the new normal. To limit yourself to just your relationship with God vertically, not building relationships with others in His name horizontally, is to limit your own personal Christian experience. We've not been instructed to pray, "My Father which art in heaven." It is, "Our Father which art in heaven" (Matthew 6:9 KJV). You will experience more of God by connecting with His purposes through His people than you could ever experience on your own.

SPIRITUAL ISOLATION

One of the issues we face today in our compartmentalized, short-ened-attention-span society is a reduction in personal relationships with others. We've traded long conversations for social media posts. We've traded "life on life" for "like on like." Unfortunately, in this process, we've likewise reduced our capacity for knowing God collectively and experiencing Him with and through others.

Scripture shows us something else we've reduced—the involvement of the Holy Spirit in our gatherings and in the impact of our ministries. In the early church movement, the collective power of those who came together to worship the Lord, learn of His teachings, and fellowship was made evident in all they did—not just externally in their influence over the culture itself, but also internally in their dealings with one another. We get a glimpse into this time in Acts 4.

> After they prayed, the place where they were meeting was shaken. And they were all filled with the Holy Spirit and spoke the word of God boldly. All the believers were one in heart and mind. No one claimed that any of their possessions was their own, but they shared everything they had. With great power the apostles continued to testify to the resurrection of the Lord Jesus. And God's grace was so powerfully at work in them all that there were no needy persons among them (verses 31-34 NIV).

Not only did the building where they were meeting literally shake, but the people in the building boldly spoke of God to those around them. It was when they came together that they became of one heart and mind. Accompanying that unity was "great power" and "God's grace."

Years ago, we had a family in our congregation whose son was suffering from a brain tumor that had grown so large that the doctors could not distinguish between where the tumor ended and where the young boy's brain stem began. There was no way to remove the entirety of the tumor without affecting the brain stem, which would permanently disable him for the rest of his life. But this family did not give up with the doctor's pronouncement. Instead, they mobilized a prayer chain through the members of the church so that someone was praying at every moment, through every hour, every day. The body of Christ came together to collectively call on God for a miracle in this young boy's life.

I'm happy to say that not long after this prayer chain began, the surgeons decided to try one more time to remove the tumor. When they had completed the surgery, they happily told the parents that they were able to remove the entire tumor without having to touch the brain stem at all.

Hundreds of people called on God on behalf of this young boy, and through their collective effort of love, prayer, and petitions, the Holy Spirit enabled the surgeons to do what they had previously determined they could not do.

This story is such a great reminder of why you should never be willing to live your life as an unattached Christian. Yes, God hears your prayers and answers them. Yes, you can know God yourself through seeking Him and abiding in Him. But there is something special of such great magnitude and such great implication that comes when we come to God together. We need to experience Him together to know the fullness of His power.

Let me put it another way: God's involvement with you increases as your involvement with His people increases.

Far too many believers are like teenagers living in their parents' home. They want their own room. They want their own television. They want their own iPad. They want their own phone. All the while they shut and lock their bedroom door, going off alone. But then they'll pop their head out once in a while and ask, "What's for dinner?" In other words, they want the convenience when it comes to corporate living arrangements, but they don't want to be disturbed by anyone.

What a lot of people today want is nothing more than convenience when it comes to the kingdom of God. God must hear a litany of similar prayers: "God, help me. Bless me. Meet my need. Do this for me." But how often does He hear, "Use me as a vehicle of ministry to someone else in Your name, for their good and Your glory"? Is that a prayer you pray every day? If it's not, I want to encourage you to begin praying it and watching how God responds.

You limit your experience with God when you live in spiritual isolation.

It is in the conjoining of ethnicities, races, cultures, genders, classes, backgrounds, skills, and histories that God strengthens His body to carry out His kingdom agenda. Can you imagine a football team with only quarterbacks? Or a baseball team with only catchers? Neither of those teams would even make it to the end of the game. This is because sports teams need the diversity, differences, and strengths of many to progress on the field. We in the body of Christ are no different.

The presence of connectivity in your spiritual walk will increase your knowledge and experience of God. The goal of God in His kingdom agenda is corporate impact, not merely individual impact. This is why He has chosen to gift us all differently and uniquely for the intended purposes He wants us to fulfill. It is in the carrying out of our gifts that we, as a whole, grow stronger. Paul speaks of this in Ephesians 4, where he writes,

Christ himself gave the apostles, the prophets, the evangelists, the pastors and teachers, to equip his people for works of service, so that the body of Christ may be built up until we all reach unity in the faith and in the knowledge of the Son of God and become mature, attaining to the whole measure of the fullness of Christ (verses 11-13 NIV).

He specifically states, "Until we all reach unity in the faith and in the knowledge of the Son of God." God doesn't want you growing spiritually while the person He's placed next to you remains stagnant. He doesn't want some within His body maturing while others remain carnal. That would be like a football coach wanting some of his players to work out and the others to eat pizza and watch Netflix all week long. A team is only as strong as its weakest players. And while God has compassion for each individual and their personal growth—and we are not to compare ourselves with others—He also has an agenda He desires to manifest on earth. This agenda involves His glory as the goal. It is only in our collective health, strength, and spiritual maturity that we can carry out the ultimate agenda of our Lord in history. And this collective health is largely dependent upon the willingness and intentionality of each believer to live as part of a collective whole.

Take the business world, for example. In business, the bottom line for one year often dictates the following year's budget and expansion. If the bottom line doesn't produce much margin of growth, then the next year's expansion will most often be limited. And if it produces a loss, then there can also be cutbacks in departments, budgets, and personnel. Thus, the collective health of the overall organization affects individuals in often drastic ways.

Unfortunately, we often neglect the intention necessary to produce gains in our collective health as the body of Christ. As a result, we continue to stand by on the sidelines, witnessing our culture devolve into a dearth of morality, and we suffer the results of the mutual mess.

I hate to tell you this so bluntly, but God is not satisfied just because you enjoyed a sermon or listened to the choir sing. He's not satisfied just because you showed up at church or joined a small group. God wants you to show how much you desire to know Him by being willing to invest in the lives of those around you, in His name. That's more than a handshake or a hello. That's opening up to others, being both vulnerable and authentic with those around you in such a way that you foster an atmosphere of mutual trust, commitment, growth, and service.

The testimony of the family with their son suffering from a brain tumor—how God supernaturally intervened to have it removed when the doctors said it was impossible—ought not to be abnormal. That shouldn't be something that happens once in a blue moon. No, the body of Christ has full access to the Creator of the universe, and when we collectively seek His heart, we access both His authority and His power. Just like the early church, we should be witnessing God's hand at work everywhere.

Membership in a church does not automatically equate to relationship. In order to fully experience the active involvement of God in your life, you must hold the relationships obtained through that membership in high regard and in true alignment. You must recognize that we need one another—not only to hold ourselves accountable to lives of purity, but also to offer encouragement and strength in times of need. And we are all to align ourselves under God's overarching rule in an effort to carry out His will on earth.

Scripture is clear that Jesus Christ is the head of the collective members of His body. Therefore, the job of Jesus' body, each one of us, is to reflect the dictates of our head, Jesus Christ. To do anything else is dysfunctional. To do anything else produces chaos, confusion, and pain. Only when we are properly aligned under the goals, visions, and directives of Jesus do we fully function as we were designed to function.

MEMBERS OF ONE BODY

Paul breaks down the concept for us of the body and its members in 1 Corinthians 12. The word *body* is used 18 times in this chapter and is often accompanied by the word *member*.

When Paul speaks of the "body," he is referencing the whole frame. When he speaks about the "members," he is talking about the individual parts that are attached to and comprise the whole frame. We actually get our term *membership* from this concept. The individual members—each one of us—have been created to implement the dictates of the brain, Jesus Christ, on behalf of the body.

Membership involves becoming a functionally attached part of a particular assembly in order to fulfill a certain responsibility. This is done so that the full body might function as the head intended it to function.

Membership does not mean your only responsibility is to sit, soak, and sour. Nor does it mean your sole contribution is to warm a pew or show up to different events. Rather, it means to identify and be functionally involved with a body of believers who are learning together to live under the lordship and rulership of Jesus. This is done both locally and globally.

It can also be done in many ways outside of a church body, such as in a small group, online group, missions experience, or nonprofit organization. While the local church body has been established as the primary point of contact and belonging for the body of Christ, membership and its responsibilities can extend beyond those four walls while simultaneously maintaining involvement within them.

Through 1 Corinthians 12, we come to understand that we can deepen our relationship with God by attachment to others. If you are detached from the other members of the body of Christ, there will be a decrease in the flow of God's relationship with you.

Let me illustrate this through a graphic visual: If I were to chop off my hand and set it on the pulpit while I went on preaching, the fact that my hand is located in the same building with my body would be meaningless. It would be meaningless for both my hand and my body—both would lose. My hand would lose because it wouldn't get the benefit of the rest of my body nor the flow of the blood it needs. And the rest of my body would lose because it wouldn't get the benefit of my hand. I would limit both my body and my hand by disconnecting them, even if they are hanging out in the same vicinity.

God has given each of us something to contribute to the greater good, but we need to be connected in order to effectively carry it out. We read this in 1 Corinthians 12:7, which says, "To each one is given the manifestation of the Spirit for the common good." The Holy Spirit is like the blood flowing through the body. He transfers God's life to the various parts of the body. But if my hand is disconnected from my arm, it doesn't get the transfer of life. Neither do we get the full manifestation of the Spirit in our lives when we are disconnected from one another. God's flow moves through connectivity—not just through our vertical connection with Him, but also through our horizontal connection with one another.

Paul goes deeper into this visual when he writes,

> Even as the body is one and yet has many members, and all the members of the body, though they are many, are one body, so also is Christ. For by one Spirit we were all baptized into one body, whether Jews or Greeks, whether slaves or free, and we were all made to drink of one Spirit.

> For the body is not one member, but many. If the foot says, "Because I am not a hand, I am not a part of the body," it is not for this reason any the less a part of the body. And if the ear says, "Because I am not an eye, I am not a part of the body," it is not for this reason any the less a part of the body. If the whole body were an eye, where would the hearing be? If the whole were hearing, where would the sense of smell be? But now God has placed the members, each one of them, in the body, just as He desired. If they were all one member, where would the body be? But now there are many members, but one body (verses 12-20).

This is such a perfect illustration of how we are made to function, because it is one we can all understand. If the whole body were an eye, we wouldn't be able to function. If the whole body were an ear, we wouldn't be able to function. Yet an eye or an ear, as part of the body, is no less important and critical than the small toe or the spleen. Each part is essential in carrying out the dictates of the head.

You are a critical part in the body of Christ. You are an important piece of God's overarching plan. When you remove yourself from functioning connectivity with others in Christ's body, then we feel the loss. It takes all the members of the body to make up the body. Just ask anyone with type 1 diabetes how important the pancreas is. Or ask anyone on dialysis how important the kidneys are. Ask any blind or deaf person how important the eyes and ears are. Then you will get a greater understanding of how important you are to the remaining members of the body of Christ. Paul makes it clear that the church grows properly and maximizes its spiritual potential when every member is making its proper contribution.

I say this humbly as a preacher, but the purpose of the church is not merely to provide a place to hear sermons or sing songs. The purpose of the church is to provide an environment for linkage with one another. It is a place where we come together, carrying out our various roles, while resultantly experiencing God more deeply in our lives. The kingdom of God and the church of Jesus Christ do not need more fans who merely sit in the stands (i.e., pews) as spectators and critique what's happening on the field. They need players on the field who are functionally engaged in building up the body of Christ.

The believer who doesn't think that they need the family of God is thinking they are something they are not (Galatians 6:3). Our unity with Jesus fleshed out in our unity with one another is critical for both the plan and the program of God. When God does not see you investing in the lives of others, He has allowed Himself the freedom to limit His experiential connection with you. If you are a Christian who cannot invest in the well-being of other Christians, you have chosen to limit God's flow to you simply because you are not an only child in this home.

An only child is often spoiled because they never have to share. But God doesn't have any only children. He has established a family comprised of many members whom He has uniquely gifted through His Spirit to benefit one another. That being so, it is absolutely critical that believers connect with one another. It is also critical that we learn to value one another. God's Word tells us that each one of us is valuable, and His truth is to be our guide. Nothing else.

Did you know this is one reason why Satan seeks to cause disunity? He wants disunity because He knows it will lessen God's involvement in our lives. God, by His very nature, is a unified being. Yet when we are fussing and fighting all the time, or when we are neglecting others in His body, we are not modeling His image in which we were created. This impacts our relationship with God. The Bible says that if a husband and wife are not getting along with understanding and a sense of value, then the husband's prayers are hindered (1 Peter 3:7).

This truth that our horizontal relationship with others impacts the experience of our vertical relationship with God shows up in so many places throughout Scripture. Yet it's something we don't often talk about, preach about, teach about, or write about. I don't know why, but we don't. And as a result, we are not truly experiencing the full manifestation of God's presence in our individual lives and families nor in our churches, communities, and nation.

Paul emphasizes God's prescribed value for each of us when he says, "God has so composed the body, giving more abundant honor to that member which lacked, so that there may be no division in the body, but that the members may have the same care for one another. And if one member suffers, all the members suffer with it; if one member is honored, all the members rejoice with it" (1 Corinthians 12:24-26).

The goal of our connectivity is summed up in those verses. We are to "care for one another." The Christian life is to be all about caring. True, we can't care for everyone, but that's why he writes about caring for "one another." We are each to care for those around us, starting with those who are a part of our local church family and then extending to those God puts on our paths (Galatians 6:10). When each of us is connected to someone else, and that someone is connected to someone else—ultimately, the entire body is connected. This involves listening, helping, serving, praying for someone, being in a small group—any number of things. But none of that can happen unless we take the risk to functionally and intentionally connect with other members of Christ's body.

When you connect with the family of God, He is positioned to give you more of an experiential relationship with Him. When you become a conduit for God's love, not just a cul-de-sac, you are positioned to experience more of Him.

We're all familiar with HOV (high-occupancy vehicle) lanes. The HOV lanes are designated for those people who are not traveling alone. If you are driving alone, then you cannot get into the faster-moving HOV lane without being penalized. A police officer will write you a ticket for being in that lane all by yourself. This is because the HOV lane is for high-occupancy vehicles only. It is a somewhat private route which allows you to bypass a large amount of traffic, but only when you have someone else riding with you.

God's got a special lane for people who are in fellowship with others as well. This is a lane that allows you to travel into the depths of knowing and experiencing Him far beyond your individual capacity. But this lane is reserved for those believers in His body who intentionally, authentically, and vulnerably connect with one another in His name in order to bring His rule to bear on earth. Knowing God is never to be considered a solitary pursuit. Rather, the power of knowing God can only be fully found in the collective presence of His people.

The Urban Alternative

The Urban Alternative (TUA) equips, empowers, and unites Christians to impact *individuals, families, churches,* and *communities* through a thoroughly kingdom agenda worldview. In teaching truth, we seek to transform lives.

The core cause of the problems we face in our personal lives, homes, churches, and societies is a spiritual one; therefore, the only way to address it is spiritually. We've tried a political, social, economic, and even a religious agenda.

It's time for a **Kingdom agenda**.

> *The Kingdom agenda can be defined as the visible manifestation of the comprehensive rule of God over every area of life.*

The unifying central theme throughout the Bible is the glory of God and the advancement of His kingdom. The conjoining thread from Genesis to Revelation—from beginning to end—is focused on one thing: God's glory through advancing God's kingdom.

When you do not have that theme, the Bible becomes disconnected stories that are great for inspiration but seem unrelated in purpose and direction. The Bible exists to share God's movement in history toward the establishment and expansion of His kingdom, highlighting the connectivity throughout which is the kingdom. Understanding that increases the relevancy of this several-thousand-year-old manuscript to your day-to-day living, because the kingdom is not only then; it is now.

The absence of the kingdom's influence in our personal and family lives, churches, and communities has led to a deterioration of immense proportions in our world:

- People live segmented, compartmentalized lives because they lack God's kingdom worldview.
- Families disintegrate because they exist for their own satisfaction rather than for the kingdom.
- Churches are limited in the scope of their impact because they fail to comprehend that the goal of the church is not the church itself, but the kingdom.
- Communities have nowhere to turn to find real solutions for real people who have real problems because the church has become divided, ingrown, and unable to transform the cultural landscape in any relevant way.

The kingdom agenda offers us a way to see and live life with a solid hope by optimizing the solutions of heaven. When God, and His rule, is no longer the final and authoritative standard under which all else falls, order and hope leaves with Him. But the reverse of that is true as well: As long as you have God, you have hope. If God is still in the picture, and as long as His agenda is still on the table, it's not over.

Even if relationships collapse, God will sustain you. Even if finances dwindle, God will keep you. Even if dreams die, God will revive you. As long as God, and His rule, is still the overarching rule in your life, family, church, and community, there is always hope.

Our world needs the King's agenda. Our churches need the King's agenda. Our families need the King's agenda.

In many major cities, there is a loop that drivers can take when they want to get somewhere on the other side of the city but don't necessarily want to head straight through downtown. This loop will take you close enough to the city so that you can see its towering buildings and skyline, but not close enough to actually experience it.

This is precisely what we, as a culture, have done with God. We have put Him on the "loop" of our personal, family, church, and community lives. He's close enough to be at hand should we need Him in an emergency but far enough away that He can't be the center of who we are.

We want God on the "loop," not the King of the Bible who comes downtown into the very heart of our ways. Leaving God on the "loop" brings about dire consequences as we have seen in our own lives and with others. But when we make God, and His rule, the centerpiece of all we think, do, or say, it is then that we will experience Him in the way He longs to be experienced by us.

He wants us to be kingdom people with kingdom minds set on fulfilling His kingdom's purposes. He wants us to pray, as Jesus did, "Not my will, but Thy will be done." Because His is the kingdom, the power, and the glory.

There is only one God, and we are not Him. As King and Creator,

God calls the shots. It is only when we align ourselves underneath His comprehensive hand that we will access His full power and authority in all spheres of life: personal, familial, church, and community.

As we learn how to govern ourselves under God, we then transform the institutions of family, church, and society from a biblically based kingdom worldview.

Under Him, we touch heaven and change earth.

To achieve our goal, we use a variety of strategies, approaches, and resources for reaching and equipping as many people as possible.

BROADCAST MEDIA

Millions of individuals experience *The Alternative with Dr. Tony Evans* through the daily radio broadcast playing on nearly 1,400 RADIO outlets and in over 130 countries. The broadcast can also be seen on several television networks, and is viewable online at TonyEvans.org. You can also listen or view the daily broadcast by downloading the Tony Evans app for free in the App store. Over 18,000,000 message downloads/streams occur each year.

LEADERSHIP TRAINING

The Tony Evans Training Center (TETC) facilitates educational programming that embodies the ministry philosophy of Dr. Tony Evans as expressed through the kingdom agenda. The training courses focus on leadership development and discipleship in the following five tracks:

- Bible and theology
- personal growth
- family and relationships
- church health and leadership development
- society and community impact strategies

The TETC program includes courses for both local and online students. Furthermore, TETC programming includes course work for nonstudent attendees. Pastors, Christian leaders, and Christian laity, both local and at a distance, can seek out The Kingdom Agenda Certificate for personal, spiritual, and professional development. For more information, visit: tonyevanstraining.org.

The Kingdom Agenda Pastors (KAP) provides a *viable network* for *like-minded pastors* who embrace the Kingdom Agenda philosophy. Pastors have the opportunity to go deeper with Dr. Tony Evans as they are given greater biblical knowledge, practical applications, and resources to impact individuals, families, churches, and communities. KAP welcomes senior and associate pastors of all churches. KAP also offers an annual Summit held each year in Dallas with intensive seminars, workshops, and resources.

Pastors' Wives Ministry, founded by Dr. Lois Evans, provides *counsel, encouragement,* and *spiritual resources* for pastors' wives as they serve with their husbands in the ministry. A primary focus of the ministry is the KAP Summit that offers senior pastors' wives a safe place to *reflect, renew,* and *relax* along with training in personal development, spiritual growth, and care for their emotional and physical well-being.

COMMUNITY AND CULTURAL INFLUENCE

National Church Adopt-A-School Initiative (NCAASI) prepares churches across the country to impact communities by using public schools as the primary vehicle for effecting positive social change in urban youth and families. Leaders of churches, school districts, faith-based organizations, and other nonprofit organizations are equipped with the knowledge and tools to forge partnerships and build strong social service delivery systems. This training is based on the comprehensive church-based community impact strategy conducted by Oak Cliff Bible Fellowship. It addresses such areas as economic development, education, housing, health revitalization, family renewal, and racial reconciliation. We assist churches in tailoring the model to meet specific needs of their communities while simultaneously addressing the spiritual and moral frame of reference. Training events are held annually in the Dallas area at Oak Cliff Bible Fellowship.

Athlete's Impact (AI) exists as an outreach both into and through the sports arena. Coaches are the most influential factor in young people's lives, even ahead of their parents. With the growing rise of fatherlessness in our culture, more young people are looking to their coaches for guidance, character development, practical needs, and hope. After coaches on the influencer scale fall athletes. Athletes (whether professional or amateur) influence younger athletes and kids within their spheres of impact. Knowing this, we have made it our aim to equip and train coaches and athletes on how to live out and utilize their God-given roles for the benefit of the kingdom. We aim to do this through our iCoach App as well as resources such as *The Playbook: A Life Strategy Guide for Athletes.*

Tony Evans Films ushers in positive life change through compelling video-shorts, animation, and feature-length films. We seek to build kingdom disciples through the power of story. We use a variety of platforms for viewer consumption and have more than 35,000,000 digital views. We also merge video-shorts and film with relevant Bible study materials to bring people to the saving knowledge of Jesus Christ and to strengthen the body of Christ worldwide. Tony Evans Films released our first feature-length film, *Kingdom Men Rising*, in April 2019, in more than 800 theaters nationwide, in partnership with Lifeway Films.

RESOURCE DEVELOPMENT

We are fostering lifelong learning partnerships with the people we serve by providing a variety of published materials. Dr. Evans has published more than 100 unique titles based on over 40 years of preaching in booklet, book, or Bible study format. He also holds the honor of writing and publishing the first full-Bible commentary and study Bible by an African-American, released in 2019.

For more information, and a complimentary copy of Dr. Evans' devotional newsletter, call (800) 800-3222 *or* write TUA at P.O. Box 4000, Dallas, TX 75208, *or* visit us online www.TonyEvans.org.

Notes

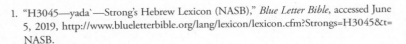

1. "H3045—yada'—Strong's Hebrew Lexicon (NASB)," *Blue Letter Bible*, accessed June 5, 2019, http://www.blueletterbible.org/lang/lexicon/lexicon.cfm?Strongs=H3045&t=NASB.

2. Erin Fothergill, et al., *Persistent Metabolic Adaptation Six Years After* The Biggest Loser *Competition* (study), May 2, 2016, http://onlinelibrary.wiley.com/doi/full/10.1002/oby.21538, as referenced in "Weight Loss vs. Fat Loss: Lessons from *The Biggest Loser*," *InBody*, June 9, 2016, http://inbodyusa.com/blogs/inbodyblog/123099905-weight-loss-vs-fat-loss-lessons-from-the-biggest-loser.

3. "G1922—epignōsis—Strong's Greek Lexicon (NASB)," *Blue Letter Bible*, accessed June 18, 2019, http://www.blueletterbible.org/lang/lexicon/lexicon.cfm?Strongs=G1922&t=NASB.

4. "H3045—yada'—Strong's Hebrew Lexicon (NASB)."

5. *Lexico*, s.v. "resolution," accessed June 18, 2019, http://www.lexico.com/en/definition/resolution.

GET TO KNOW GOD AS HE REALLY IS

Dr. Tony Evans believes knowing God fully should be everyone's life pursuit. In this highly practical, six-session DVD series based on his book *The Power of Knowing God*, he shares his strategy for living victoriously as a child of God.

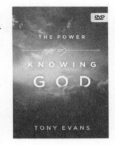

God wants more than a fan club. He wants an intimate relationship with you. Through personal storytelling and in-depth scriptural studies, Dr. Evans will equip you with the right tools for success in pursuing a personal and authentic relationship with the Savior that goes beyond church attendance, reading the Bible, and attending study groups.

Experience the fullness of life when you walk step by step with God.

Complete your DVD experience with *The Power of Knowing God Interactive Workbook*.

ARE YOU LIVING THE LIFE YOU WERE CREATED FOR?

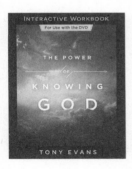

God has called you to know Him and experience Him. And He wants you to know Him beyond intellect, emotion, and action. He is your friend, but He is interested in so much more. He wants an intimate relationship with you.

In this companion to Dr. Tony Evans' *The Power of Knowing God* DVD, he shares with you his strategies for creating an authentic connection with God. This comprehensive resource provides insightful stories and practical applications to help you pursue a true relationship with God. You'll find this full of relevant Scripture passages, reflective questions that spark conversation, and activities for personal growth.

Use in a group or on your own as you make knowing God your life's pursuit... and experience the fullness of living the life He created you for.

Building kingdom disciples.

At **The Urban Alternative,** our heart is to build kingdom disciples—a vision that starts with the individual and expands to the family, the church and the nation. The nearly 50-year teaching ministry of Tony Evans has allowed us to reach a world in need with:

The Alternative – Our flagship radio program brings hope and comfort to an audience of millions on over 1,400 radio outlets across the country.

tonyevans.org – Our library of teaching resources provides solid Bible teaching through the inspirational books and sermons of Tony Evans.

Tony Evans Training Center – Experience the adventure of God's Word with our online classroom, providing at-your-own-pace courses for your PC or mobile device. Visit tonyevanstraining.org.

Tony Evans app – This popular resource for finding inspiration on-the-go has had over 20,000,000 launches. It's packed with audio and video clips, devotionals, Scripture readings and dozens of other tools.

tonyevans.org

MORE GREAT
HARVEST HOUSE BOOKS BY
DR. TONY EVANS

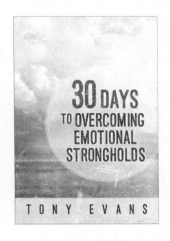

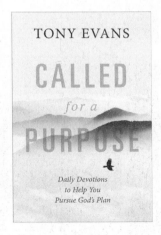

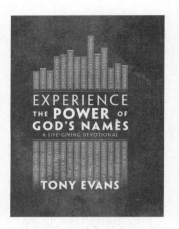

EXPERIENCE
THE **POWER** OF
GOD'S NAMES
A LIFE-GIVING DEVOTIONAL

TONY EVANS

EXPERIENCING
GOD
TOGETHER
How Your Connection with Others Deepens
Your Relationship with God

TONY EVANS

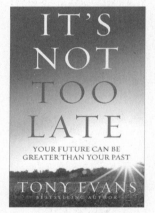

IT'S
NOT
TOO
LATE

YOUR FUTURE CAN BE
GREATER THAN YOUR PAST

TONY EVANS
BESTSELLING AUTHOR

THE **POWER** OF
GOD'S NAMES

TONY EVANS
BESTSELLING AUTHOR

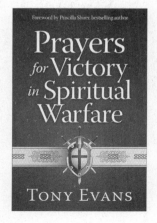

Foreword by Priscilla Shirer, bestselling author

Prayers
for Victory
in Spiritual
Warfare

TONY EVANS

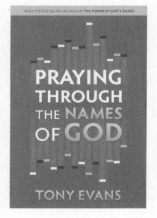

FROM THE BESTSELLING AUTHOR OF *THE POWER OF GOD'S NAMES*

**PRAYING
THROUGH
THE NAMES
OF GOD**

TONY EVANS

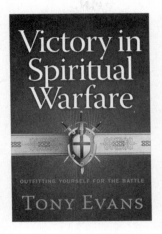

Victory in Spiritual Warfare

OUTFITTING YOURSELF FOR THE BATTLE

TONY EVANS

TONY EVANS

STRONGER TOGETHER,

WEAKER APART

POWERFUL PRAYERS TO UNITE US IN LOVE

watch your mouth

Understanding the Power of the Tongue

TONY EVANS

Bestselling author of The Power of God's Names

TONY EVANS

YOUR COMEBACK

YOUR PAST DOESN'T HAVE TO DETERMINE YOUR FUTURE

To learn more about Harvest House books and
to read sample chapters, visit our website:

www.harvesthousepublishers.com

HARVEST HOUSE PUBLISHERS
EUGENE, OREGON